Routledge Revivals

Cases and Materials on Sale of Goods

This book, first published in 1982, focuses on a specific area of commercial law: the Sale of Goods Act. The book contains key cases and statutes relating to the sale of goods, each prefaced by a contextualising introduction. Notes and questions are also included, as are the full texts of the Sale of Goods Act 1979 and the relevant parts of the Unfair Contract Terms Act 1977.

Cases and Materials on Sale of Goods

John Adams

Routledge
Taylor & Francis Group

First published in 1982
by Croom Helm Ltd

This edition first published in 2021 by Routledge
2 Park Square, Milton Park, Abingdon, Oxon, OX14 4RN
and by Routledge
605 Third Avenue, New York, NY 10017

Routledge is an imprint of the Taylor & Francis Group, an informa business

Publisher's Note
The publisher has gone to great lengths to ensure the quality of this reprint but points out that some imperfections in the original copies may be apparent.

Disclaimer
The publisher has made every effort to trace copyright holders and welcomes correspondence from those they have been unable to contact.

A Library of Congress record exists under LCCN: 81208124

ISBN 13: 978-1-032-00534-8 (hbk)
ISBN 13: 978-1-003-17461-5 (ebk)

DOI: 10.4324/9781003174615

John Adams

Cases and Materials on Sale of Goods

CROOM HELM
London & Canberra

Croom Helm Ltd, 2-10 St John's Road, London SW11

British Library Cataloguing in Publication Data

Adams, John
Cases and materials on sale of goods – (Croom Helm study guides to commercial law)
1. Sales – Great Britain – Cases
I. Title
344.106'72'0264 KD1650.A7

ISBN 0-7099-0509-2

Printed and bound in Great Britain
by Billing and Sons Limited
Guildford, London, Oxford, Worcester

Contents

Acknowledgements

I would like to thank Professor Clive Schmitthoff for his valuable suggestions, Professor Aubrey Diamond and the staff of the Institute of Advanced Legal Studies for their helpfulness and efficiency without which the compilation of this book would have been much more difficult, and Mrs Lydia Foreman for typing the manuscript quickly and accurately. Needless to say, the responsibility for errors and omissions is entirely mine.

Foreword

The publication of this series of *Study Guides to Commercial Law* will be welcomed by students and teachers alike. It fills a gap in English legal literature. It is of the utmost importance that the students should be introduced to the use of primary material contained in the cases and statutes. These Study Guides give them an opportunity of supplementing their textbook reading by reference to the sources of law. Concise, well selected, competently edited and moderately priced source books should be companion volumes for every serious-minded student of commercial law which, after all, is the most lively and, from the practical point of view, most rewarding branch of our legal system.

The first book in this series, *Cases and Materials on Sale of Goods*, is a model of what such a companion book should be. Edited by a distinguished scholar and experienced law teacher, it enables the student to analyse topics which, by necessity, are treated only briefly in the textbooks. Each section is introduced by a statement of law which highlights, in clear and easily understandable language, the outstanding features of the subject. Then follow extracts from leading cases which are selected with consummate skill and are truly representative of the topics treated in the section. At the end notes and questions are added. It is a particular merit of the book that the text of the Sale of Goods Act 1979 and the Unfair Contract Terms Act 1977 is included. The work is clearly the result of years of teaching experience and is skilfully adapted to the needs of the student who not only wishes to pass his examinations but who intends to prepare himself conscientiously for his professional career.

This series of Study Guides will also be welcomed by students outside Great Britain, particularly in the other countries which have founded their legal system on the common law. Not all libraries, public and private, include all the collections of cases referred to in these volumes. Here the Study Guides will be of considerable help and assistance.

CLIVE M. SCHMITTHOFF

Preface

The point of this series is that each title should concentrate on a specific area of commercial law and try to illuminate the difficulties within that area. It is impossible in a small compass to provide cases and materials on every aspect of sale of goods which students may be required to study in any particular course – particularly in view of the widely differing courses in which the subject is studied. The focus of this particular title is the Sale of Goods Act itself. Consequently, little attempt is made to place the Act in context. For example, the problems inherent in private law remedies for consumer protection are not studied (consumer protection may, of course, form the subject matter of a later title). However, to the extent that the quality warranties in themselves involve fundamental problems of products liability which are pertinent to consumer protection, they are covered. Similarly contracting out is covered, because this is raised by the Act itself. Again no attempt is made to cover relevant areas of general contract law, save as problems are raised by the Act itself.

Selection of material was based purely on the practical consideration of what would be likely to be of use to the greatest number of students. What I have tried to concentrate on are areas students are most likely to come across and find difficult. I have tried to make the linking text clear but I hope not oversimplified, and to organise the material so as to suggest connections which traditional organisation might not. Thus, frustration does not appear under discharge at the end of the book, but under 'The Exchange of Risks Effected by Formation'.

Sale of goods is a subject which most students should find interesting. I hope that this book may help to stimulate that interest.

Table of Cases

Cases which are set out in this book are indicated by bold type

Table of Statutes

Introduction

The Sale of Goods Act 1979 consolidates the amendments made from time to time to the Sale of Goods Act 1893. Apart from some minor insertions made necessary by the Unfair Contract Terms Act 1977, the 1979 Act does not make new law. Consequently, subject to any changes made by the earlier amendments, cases and comment on the interpretation of the 1893 Act continue to be relevant.

The cases and materials in this book have been selected in the hope of helping the reader to understand the principal areas of difficulty.[1] Some of the problems are simply a product of the age of the original Act. The Sale of Goods Act 1893 codified rapid developments which had taken place through case law in the course of the nineteenth century. Almost certainly, one consequence of the codification was to slow down, or even prevent, further desirable developments which might otherwise have taken place through case law. It is also to be borne in mind that the Act was largely derived from commercial cases. That, too, leads to problems because at the present day we are increasingly thinking of consumer contracts as a separate category.[2] Nevertheless, the Act is still for the most part remarkably fit for the purposes for which it is required. Some amendments may soon result from the Lord Chancellor's reference to the Law Commission of January 1979. This is in three parts, and requires them to consider:

(a) Whether the undertakings as to the quality and fitness of goods implied under the law relating to the sale of goods, hire-purchase and other contracts for the supply of goods require amendment;
(b) The circumstances in which a person, to whom goods are supplied under a contract of sale, hire-purchase or other contract for the supply of goods, is entitled, where there has been a breach by the supplier of a term implied by the statute to:
    (i) reject the goods and treat the contract as repudiated;
    (ii) claim against the supplier a diminution in or extinction of the price;
    (iii) claim damages against the supplier;

DOI: 10.4324/9781003174615-1

(c) The circumstances in which, by reason of the Act, a buyer loses the right to reject the goods.

The Commission has not yet reported.

1 Is It a Sale of Goods?

The Sale of Goods Act 1979, as we might expect, applies to sales of goods and nothing but sales of goods. A sale of goods is defined by s. 2(1) of the Act as 'a contract by which the seller transfers or agrees to transfer the property in goods to the buyer for a money consideration, called the price'.[3] This definition excludes from the Act certain related contracts: (1) bailments, e.g. hire (no property is transferred); (2) barter (no price); and (3) work and materials. Whilst there would be obvious difficulties in applying the provisions of the Act to bailments such as hire, there is no very good reason why they should not be applied to contracts of barter or work and materials. Barter, it may be applied to contracts of barter, or work and materials. Barter, it may of cars, goods supplied in return for wrappers or coupons,[4] all involve barters. It might be possible to regard contracts of barter as mutual sales, the obligation on each side to pay the price being regarded as discharged by mutual accord and satisfaction on delivery of the goods.[5] Whilst that may sound a little artificial, it does have the merit of making the provisions of the Act applicable. Work and materials contracts offer no such easy solution. All that it is possible to say is that the courts at the present day have tended to assimilate the provisions applicable to these to sale of goods.[6] Historically, the distinction was important, because contracts for the sale of goods above £10 needed to be evidenced in writing or they were unenforceable,[7] whereas work and materials did not. That requirement has now been repealed,[8] but the cases on it are still cited as authorities which define the applicability of the Act. Bearing in mind, however, that a judge deciding a case on the evidence in writing provision was concerned with the possible enforcement of a contract in the absence of the evidence required by law for sales of goods, whereas a judge now will no doubt have at the forefront of his mind only the appropriateness of the Sale of Goods Act provisions to the case in hand, these old cases may not provide an entirely reliable guide. Moreover, the test set out in the leading case of *Robinson* v. *Graves*[9] leaves the judge a great deal of leeway.

DOI: 10.4324/9781003174615-2

ROBINSON v. GRAVES [1935] 1 K.B. 579

The defendant commissioned for 250 guineas a portrait of his wife-to-be, from the plaintiff, an artist. He subsequently repudiated the contract. Was this a sale of paint, canvas, etc., or a contract for work and materials?

GREER L.J.

If you find, as they did in *Lee* v. *Griffin* 1 B. & S. 272; 30 L.J. (Q.B.) 252., that the substance of the contract was the production of something to be sold . . . then that is a sale of goods. But if the substance of the contract, on the other hand, is that skill and labour have to be exercised for the production of the article and that it is only ancillary to that that there will pass from the artist to his client or customer some materials in addition to the skill involved in the production of the portrait, that does not make any difference to the result, because the substance of the contract is the skill and experience of the artist in producing the picture.

For these reasons I am of opinion that in this case the substance of the matter was an agreement for the exercise of skill and it was only incidental that some materials would have to pass from the artist to the gentleman who commissioned the portrait. For these reasons I think that this was not a contract for the sale of goods within the meaning of s. 4 of the Sale of Goods Act, 1893, but it was a contract for work and labour and materials.

Questions

1. In *Lee* v. *Griffin*[10] a dentist sued for the price of a set of false teeth he had made for a lady, alas subsequently deceased. Why was that a contract for the sale of goods? Are National Health teeth different?[11]
2. If an artist executes a painting, and it is destroyed before delivery to the person who commissioned it, is that person nevertheless liable to pay the price?[12]

Problem

A commissioned a large metal sculpture from B. The sculpture was executed and delivered to A. Unfortunately, because of a hidden flaw in the metal, the sculpture collapses. Has A any remedy?[13]

2 Formation

(1) AUCTION SALES

WARLOW v. HARRISON (1859) 1 E & E 309

The plaintiff attended an auction and bid 60 guineas for a mare. The owner bid 61 guineas and the mare was knocked down to him. The plaintiff sued the auctioneer.

MARTIN B.

Upon the facts of the case, it seems to us that the plaintiff is entitled to recover. In a sale by auction there are three parties, viz. the owner of the property to be sold, the auctioneer, and the portion of the public who attend to bid, which of course includes the highest bidder. In this, as in most cases of sales by auction, the owner's name was not disclosed: he was a concealed principal. The name of the auctioneers, of whom the defendant was one, alone was published; and the sale was announced by them to be 'without reserve'. This, according to all the cases both at law and equity, means that neither the vendor nor any person in his behalf shall bid at the auction, and that the property shall be sold to the highest bidder, whether the sum bid be equivalent to the real value or not; *Thornett* v. *Haines* (15 M. & W. 367). We cannot distinguish the case of an auctioneer putting up property for sale upon such a condition from the case of the loser of property offering a reward, or that of a railway company publishing a time table stating the times when, and the places to which, the trains run. It has been decided that the person giving the information advertised for, or a passenger taking a ticket, may sue as upon a contract with him; *Denton* v. *Great Northern Railway Company* (5 E. & B. 860). Upon the same principle, it seems to us that the highest bona fide bidder at an auction may sue the auctioneer as upon a contract that the sale shall be without reserve. We think the auctioneer who puts the property up for sale upon such a condition pledges himself that the sale shall be without reserve; or, in other words, contracts that it shall be so; and that this contract is made with the highest bona fide bidder; and, in case of a breach of it, that he has a right of action against the auctioneer. The case is not at all affected by the 17th section of the Statute of Frauds, which relates only to direct sales, and not to contracts relating to or connected with them. Neither does it seem to us material whether the owner, or person on his behalf, bid with the knowledge or privity of the auctioneer. We think the auctioneer has contracted that the sale shall be without reserve; and that the contract is broken upon a bid

DOI: 10.4324/9781003174615-3

being made by or on behalf of the owner, whether it be during the time when the property is under the hammer, or it be the last bid upon which the article is knocked down; in either case the sale is not 'without reserve', and the contract of the auctioneer is broken. We entertain no doubt that the owner may, at any time before the contract is legally complete, interfere and revoke the auctioneer's authority: but he does so at his peril; and, if the auctioneer has contracted any liability in consequence of his employment and the subsequent revocation or conduct of the owner, he is entitled to be indemnified.

Questions

1. How could there be a breach of contract here (see s.57(2))?
2. The seller can withdraw up to the fall of the hammer.[14] Was the seller in *Warlow* v. *Harrison* not exercising his right of withdrawal by another means, i.e. by bidding a price no-one else would better?
3. If the answer to Question 2 is 'yes', what is the purpose of s. 57(3)? Would that section apply whether it was (a) seller suing buyer, or (b) buyer suing seller?
4. If the seller can withdraw the lot before the fall of the hammer, what is the purpose of s. 57(4)?

(2) THE EXCHANGE OF RISKS EFFECTED BY FORMATION

A contract for the sale of goods involves an exchange of risks. Before the contract, the seller takes the chance of the goods deterioriating, or perishing or of the market price falling. After the contract the buyer prima facie takes the chance of the goods deterioriating or perishing, or of the market price falling. Once we have realised this we will see that it generates a number of questions which the law must attempt to answer. At what point does this exchange of risks take place – with the transfer of possession of the goods under the contract or on some other event? (See Chapter 3.) Do we hold the seller liable for all mishaps before risks are exchanged, or just some? On this question the law produces a somewhat crude distinction between total loss of specific goods which will generally excuse the seller, and mere deterioration below the standard contemplated by the contract for which the seller may be liable under the quality warranties. (See Chapter 5.) The risk of the market rising after the contract, so that the bargain is less good than it would have been, is borne by the seller, just as the buyer has the risk of the market falling after the contract.

In what we might term the paradigm case of a sale of goods the parties agree on the subject matter, its description and quality, its quantity and its price. In fact, however, parties do not always wish to effect the exchange of risks implicit in such an agreement. They may wish, for example, to leave quantities uncertain, so that the risk of stockpiling unwanted goods remains with the seller – the classical form of requirements contract used, for example, in the motor industry.[15] Or they may not wish to exchange the risks of market fluctuations implicit in fixing a price for the goods. The further an agreement has departed from the paradigm case, the more reluctance there has been to accept that it could be a contract recognised by law at all. The problems of this are examined here.

(a) Non-specification of quantity and price terms

PERCIVAL v. LONDON COUNTY COUNCIL ASYLUMS (1918) 87 L.J.K.B. 677

The plaintiffs undertook to supply the defendants with butter to the extent that it should be ordered by the defendants at a certain price for a certain period. The defendants chose, however, to give the wretched inmates margarine (which they obtained elsewhere) and consequently ordered no butter.

ATKIN J.
These tenders have been the subject of litigation before now, and they vary in form, but one knows that it is quite common for large bodies that require supplies over a year to ask for tenders and to obtain them, and it sometimes happens that the effect of the form of the tender with an acceptance is to make a firm contract by which the purchasing body undertakes to buy all the specified material from the contractor. On the other hand, one knows that these tenders are very often in a form under which the purchasing body is not bound to give the tenderer any order at all; in other words, the contractor offers to supply goods at a price, and if the purchasing body chooses to give him an order for goods during the stipulated time, then he is under an obligation to supply the goods in accordance with the order; but apart from that nobody is bound. There is also an intermediate contract that can be made in which, although the parties are not bound to any specified quantity, yet they bind themselves to buy and to pay for all the goods that are in fact needed by them. Of course, if there is a contract such as that, then there is a binding contract which will be broken if the purchasing body in fact do[es] need some of the articles [which are] the subject of the tender, and do[es] not take them from the tenderer.

In this case it appears to me that this is a contract of the first kind.

The London County Council Committees have asked for tenders, and they have got tenders, and they have made it plain that they are under no obligation to order any of the goods, and that the tenderer on the other hand, is under an obligation to deliver the goods specified in his tender, as and when he gets orders for them. That appears to me to be the true construction of this contract, and I think that this is made plain by these words in the tender 'to supply to the Committee if and to the extent the same shall be ordered by the Committee,' and also by the other conditions.

Questions

Atkin J. calls this a 'contract'. What is the consideration for it? Is it really a standing offer, in which case could the plaintiff have withdrawn it at any time by giving notice?[16]

MAY & BUTCHER LTD v. THE KING [1934] 2 K.B. 17n

The suppliants agreed with the Controller of the Disposals Board to purchase the whole tentage which might become available for disposal up to 31 March 1923. £1000 was deposited by the suppliants as security for carrying out of the agreement. The only price term was as follows: 'The price or prices to be paid . . . shall be agreed upon from time to time between the Commission and the purchasers as the quantities of all tentage become available for disposal, and are offered to the purchasers by the Commission.'

LORD BUCKMASTER
In my opinion there never was a concluded contract between the parties. It has long been a well recognised principle of contract law that an agreement between two parties to enter into an agreement in which some critical part of the contract matter is left undetermined is no contract at all. It is of course perfectly possible for two people to contract that they will sign a document which contains all the relevant terms, but it is not open to them to agree that they will in the future agree upon a matter which is vital to the arrangement between them and has not yet been determined. It has been argued that as the fixing of the price has broken down, a reasonable price must be assumed. That depends in part upon the terms of the Sale of Goods Act, which no doubt reproduces, and is known to have reproduced, the old law upon the matter. That provides in s. 8 that 'the price in a contract of sale may be fixed by the contract, or may be left to be fixed in manner thereby agreed, or may be determined by the course of dealing between the parties. Where the price is not determined in accordance with the foregoing provisions the buyer must pay a reasonable price'; while, if the agreement is to sell goods on the terms that the price is to be fixed by the valuation of a third party, and such third party cannot or does not make such valuation, s. 9 says that the agreement is avoided. I find myself quite unable to understand the distinction between an agreement to permit the price to be fixed by a third party and an

agreement to permit the price to be fixed in the future by the two parties to the contract themselves. In principle it appears to me that they are one and the same thing. This principle is not without one or two important authorities. I think that Parker J.'s decision in *Von Hatzfeldt-Wildenburg* v. *Alexander* [1912] 1 Ch.284 really covers the whole of this dispute, although I agree that the comment upon it by Sargant L.J. in *Chillingworth* v. *Esche* [1924] 1 Ch.97, 113 more fully and accurately expresses the whole position; but the principle that you cannot agree to agree remains entirely unchanged. *Loftus* v. *Roberts* (1902) 18 Times L.R. 532 is to the same effect. The only way the appellants seek to escape from those authorities is by saying that all related to another subject-matter. If it could be shown that the different subject-matter was the cause of different principles of contract being applied, that would be an effective and relevant argument, but apart from the fact that a contract, one, for example, for the sale of land, requires the consideration of a large number of special details that are wholly unnecessary in relation to a contract for the sale of goods, and apart also from the way in which either of these contracts may be regulated by the Statute of Frauds on the one hand, or by the Sale of Goods Act on the other hand, the general underlying principles of contract are the same in each, and there is no reason why those principles should be in any way varied because of the subject-matter with which they deal. I therefore find myself quite unable to accede to the argument that the authorities to which I have referred are weakened in their application to the present case because it happens that their subject-matter is not the same.

Question

Why in the absence of agreement could the court not fix a reasonable price under s. 8 of the Sale of Goods Act? Compare *Foley* v. *Classique Coaches Ltd.*[17] See also *Smith* v. *Morgan*.[18]

(b) Frustration and mistake

If the deterioriation in, or loss of the goods, occurs after the risk is passed to the buyer, that is the end of the matter. Where it has occurred at some earlier stage the question of the seller's liability for it arises. In the most drastic case, where the goods perish altogether, the law has tended to treat the contract as avoided. Although the Act, for historical reasons, distinguishes pre-contractual perishing (mistake – s. 6) and post-contractual perishing (frustration – s. 7), really in the context of sale of goods similar considerations apply to both.[19] In both cases the law in effect makes a policy decision that the loss which has occurred has gone beyond the exchange of risks forming the subject matter of the contract.[20]

Ss. 6 and 7 are not the only sections in the Act which may relieve the seller from liability for non-delivery on the occurrence of what may loosely be termed frustrating events. S. 5(2) expressly permits sales of goods whose acquisition depends upon a contingency which may or may not happen. The question in such cases, if the worst comes to the worst, is whether or not the seller remains under a duty to deliver whatever part of the goods are in his possession. It may well be that the failure is due to a general disaster, and the seller is able to sell what goods he has more profitably elsewhere because the market has risen.

SAINSBURY LTD v. STREET [1972] 1 W.L.R. 834

The defendant agreed to sell 275 tons of feed barley to the plaintiff. The crop produced only 140 tons which he sold to a third party. The plaintiff sued for non-delivery of the 140 tons.

MACKENNA J.

Mr Rawlins argued that it was reasonable that the defendant should be freed of all his obligations under the contract if without his fault he failed to produce the whole tonnage. 275 tons (5 per cent, more or less) set an upper limit to the quantity which the plaintiffs could be compelled to take. It was reasonable, he said, that there should be a lower limit to the amount which the defendant could be compelled to deliver. In a year when the latter's yield was high, market prices would probably be low, and it would be a benefit to the plaintiffs not to be required to take more than an agreed tonnage at the contract price fixed in advance. In a year when the yield was low, as in the present case, it would be a benefit to the defendant if he were free to disregard his contract and to sell his crop to some other buyer at the higher market price. The contract should, if possible, be construed as giving him this freedom. I am not persuaded by the argument. The upper limit of 275 tons might in the circumstances of a particular case be beneficial to both parties. But even if it could be beneficial only to the buyer that is no reason for implying a term that the same figure shall serve as a lower limit to the seller's obligation to deliver, so that his failure to reach that figure, if blameless, would release him from the contract.

I must now consider the three authorities which Mr Rawlins put before me in support of his argument. The first was *Howell* v. *Coupland* (1874) L.R. 9 Q.B. 462, a decision of the Court of Queen's Bench upheld by the Court of Appeal (1876) 1 Q.B.D. 258. The headnote in the first report reads:

> Plaintiff and defendant entered into an agreement in March, whereby defendant agreed to sell and plaintiff to purchase '200 tons of regent potatoes grown on land belonging to defendant in W., at rate of £3 10s 6d per ton, to be delivered in September or October, and paid for as taken away.' In March defendant had 68 acres ready for

potatoes, which were sown, and were amply sufficient to grow more than 200 tons in an average year; but in August the potatoe blight appeared and the crop failed, so that the plaintiff was able to deliver only 80 tons. The plaintiff, having brought an action for the non-delivery of the other 120 tons: – *Held*, that the contract was for a portion of a specific crop, and was within the principle of *Taylor* v. *Caldwell* (1863) 3 B. & S. 826, 833-434, and the contract must be taken to be subject to the implied condition that the parties should be excused, if, before breach, performance becomes impossible from the perishing of the thing without default in the contractor.

Blackburn J. gave his reasons for the decision at pp. 465-6:

The principle of *Taylor* v. *Caldwell*, 3 B. & S. 826 which was followed in *Appleby* v. *Myers* (1867) L.R. 2 C.P. 651 in the Exchequer Chamber, at all events, decides that where there is a contract with respect to a particular thing, and that thing cannot be delivered owing to it perishing without any default in the seller, the delivery is excused. Of course, if the perishing were owing to any default of the seller, that would be quite another thing. But here the crop failed entirely owing to the blight, which no skill, care, or dilligence of the defendant could prevent . . . But the contract was for 200 tons of a particular crop in particular fields, and therefore there was an implied term in the contract that each party should be free if the crop perished. The property and risk had clearly not been transferred under the terms of this contract, so that the consequence of the failure of this crop is, that the bargain is off so far as the 120 tons are concerned.

It is clear from the statement of the facts in the headnote that the case raised no question about the seller's obligation to deliver the potatoes which he had in fact produced, and clear from the last sentence quoted from the judgment of Blackburn J. that it gives no support to the view that the bargain was off both as to the 120 tons and the 80 tons. There is nothing in the judgements of the Court of Appeal which touches this question.

After the decision of *Howell* v. *Coupland* the Sale of Goods Act 1893 was passed. Its relevant provisions are contained in the following sections:

5(2) There may be a contract for the sale of goods, the acquisition of which by the seller depends upon a contingency which may or may not happen.

> 6. Where there is a contract for the sale of specific goods, and the goods, without the knowledge of the seller, have perished at the time when the contract is made, the contract is void.
> 7. Where there is an agreement to sell specific goods, and subsequently the goods, without any fault on the part of the seller or buyer, perish before the risk passes to the buyer, the agreement is thereby avoided.
> 61(2). The rules of the common law, including the law merchant, save in so far as they are inconsistent with the express provisions of this Act, and in particular the rules relating to the law of principal and agent and the effect of fraud, misrepresentation, duress or coercion, mistake or other invalidating cause, shall continue to apply to contracts for the sale of goods.

The rule of *Howell* v. *Coupland*, L.R. 9 Q.B. 462 is, I think, preserved by s. 5(2). If I am wrong in that view, because the growing of a crop cannot be considered the 'acquisition' of goods within the meaning of that section, then it is preserved by s. 61(2). I do not think that it is preserved by s. 6 or 7. These sections deal with goods existing, and a crop not yet grown does not answer either description. I quote a passage from the judgement of Atkin L.J. in *In re Wait* [1927] 1 Ch. 606, 631, which was the next case cited by Mr Rawlins:

> The case of *Howell* v. *Coupland* should now be covered by section 5(2) of the Code, or, as it suggested by the learned authors of the last two editions of *Benjamin on Sale*, by section 61(2) of the Code.

The decision in *Wait*'s case does not touch the question which I have to decide, and I pass from it to the third case cited by Mr Rawlins, *Barrow, Lane and Ballard Ltd* v. *Phillip Phillips and Co. Ltd* [1929] 1 K.B. 574, a decision of Wright J. in which he applied section 6 of the Sale of Goods Act 1893 to the following facts. The plaintiffs had sold the defendants goods described as '700 bags marked E.C.P. and known as lot 7 of Chinese ground nuts in shell then lying at the National Wharves in London.' Unknown to either party there were not 700 bags then lying at the wharves but only 591, as the wharfingers or their servants had abstracted 109. The contract of sale was made on October 11. On October 12 the sellers gave the buyers a delivery order for the 700 bags and the buyers gave bills of exchange for the price. Between October 11 and December 6, more bags were abstracted, but there were still just enough to meet two delivery orders totalling 150 bags sent by the buyers to the warehouse on December 6 or 7. All the rest had gone. The sellers sued the buyers on the bills for the price of 591 bags. The buyers admitted liability for the 150 actually delivered but disputed liability for the balance. The buyers won. The following passage gives the reason for the decision at p. 583:

> Does the case come within section 6 of the Sale of Goods Act, so that it would be the same as if the whole parcel had ceased to exist? In my judgment it does. The contract here was for a parcel of 700 bags, and at the time when it was made there were only 591 bags. A contract for a parcel of 700 bags is something different from a contract for 591 bags, and the position appears to me to be in no way different from what it would have been if the whole 700 bags had ceased to exist. The result is that the parties were contracting about something which, at the date of the contract, without the knowledge or fault of either party, did not exist. To compel the buyer in those circumstances to take 591 bags would be to compel him to take something which he had not contracted to take, and would in my judgment be unjust.

If there had been no misfortune the sellers could not have compelled the buyers to take 591 bags in lieu of 700. That was not the buyer's contract. Their obligation was to take 700 bags and nothing less. Section 6 should not be so construed as to oblige them to take the lesser quantity. There are two steps in this reasoning. First there is the construction of the contract, which is held not to impose any obligation on the buyers to accept less than 700 bags. The second step is the construction of section 6. Neither part of the decision compels me to decide the present case in the defendant's favour. Because the contract in that case did not oblige the buyer to accept less than 700 bags is no reason why the implied condition in this case, which excuses the defendant from making full delivery, should be construed as excusing him from delivering the lesser quantity in fact produced if the plaintiffs are willing to accept it. The meaning of section 6 cannot affect the present case.

A passage in *Benjamin on Sale*, 7th ed. (1931), pp. 156-157 is relevant:

> It was not decided in *Howell* v. *Coupland*, L.R. 9 Q.B. 462 whether the seller might have refused delivery of the 80 tons which he in fact delivered. Blackburn J. and Quain J. seemed to have thought that he was liable to deliver what he could. On the other hand, in *Lovatt* v. *Hamilton* (1839) 5 M & W 639, when goods were sold 'to arrive' by a particular ship, and only a small part arrived in that ship, the Court of Exchequer held that the buyers were not entitled to it, as the contract was entire for the whole quantity. But this was a case of condition precedent; and it is arguable that, as the seller's excuse under section 7 is a privilege operating by way of condition subsequent he should not be entitled to excuse himself to an extent more than is necessary. The question is one of the presumed intention of the parties. When the subject matter of the sale is such an indivisible whole as a number of volumes forming one

> work, the intention would doubtless be that the seller should be wholly discharged. The case of a mere quantity of specific goods is not so clear.

I have four comments to make on this passage. (1) I would distinguish *Lovatt* v. *Hamilton*, 5 M & W 639 on the language of the contract which provided for the sale of

> 50 tons of palm oil, to arrive per Mansfield, at £32 per ton . . . In the case of non-arrival, or the vessels not having so much in after delivery of former contracts, this contract to be void.

The ship had only 7 tons in after delivery of former contracts. It was held that the buyers were not entitled to these 7 tons. The case is, I think, distinguishable. It is one thing to hold that where a contract provides that it shall be void in a certain case, this means that it shall be wholly inoperative, which is the decision in *Lovatt* v. *Hamilton*. It is another to hold that the failure of an implied condition must always operate to discharge the whole contract, which I am in effect asked to hold.

(2) I have already expressed the view that section 7 of the Sale of Goods Act 1893 is not the relevant section in a case like *Howell* v. *Coupland*, L.R. 9 Q.B. 462. The excuse is given to the seller either by a condition of the kind referred to in section 5(2) of the Act or by one implied under some provision of the common law preserved by section 61(2).

(3) The condition which excuses the defendant can be cast either in the form of a condition precedent to the existence of an obligation to deliver, or in the form of a condition subsequent to the existence of such an obligation determining the same, without affecting the substance of the matter. 'He shall be under an obligation to deliver in the future if he produces . . .' would be in form a condition precedent. 'He is under an obligation to deliver in the future but that obligation shall be discharged if he does not produce . . .' would be in form a condition subsequent. The difference is a matter of words, not of substance: see *Williston on Sales*, rev. ed. (1948), para. 8. For this reason I should not wish to rest anything, in this case at least, on the distinction between the two kinds of conditions.

(4) What is said in this passage about the presumed intention of the parties seems to me very relevant in determining what condition shall be implied. It should be a condition which will give effect to the presumed intention of reasonable men. In the case which the writer supposes it would be unreasonable to compel the buyer to accept delivery of the odd volume. This difficulty could be met in one of two ways, either by implying a condition in cases of that kind that the contract shall be wholly discharged, or by implying a condition in such cases, or indeed in all cases when the seller is excused, that the buyer shall have an option of accepting part delivery. The United States Sales Act cited in *Williston on Sales* expressly allows the buyer in case of

deterioration or partial destruction of the subject matter of a sale or contract to sell, to require such performance as remains possible.

So much for the authorities which do not, I think, oblige me to decide this case in the defendant's favour. Therefore my judgment will be for the plaintiffs for £1,050.

Note

1. If the buyer were to reject the 80 tons tendered in a case such as this, the seller would have no remedy, for under s. 30(1) Sale of Goods Act he has a right of rejection in such a case. If, on the other hand, the seller takes advantage of a favourable market which has come about because of a general crop failure, he will be liable to the buyer for not tendering the 80 tons (as we have just seen).
2. For a simpler solution to the *Barrow, Lane and Ballard* v. *Phillips and Co. Ltd* problem, see s. 28.

The meaning of 'perish'

ASFAR AND CO. v. BLUNDELL [1896] 1 Q.B. 123

A vessel carrying a cargo of dates sank to the bottom of the river Thames. The vessel was subsequently raised, and although the dates still resembled dates, they were impregnated with sewage and in such a state of fermentation as no longer to be merchantable as dates. The issue was whether or not there had been a total loss of the subject-matter of a policy of insurance (i.e. the case is not directly on ss. 6 and 7, Sale of Goods Act, but presumably on similar facts falling within those sections the court would have to confront the same issue as to whether or not there had been a total loss).

LORD ESHER M.R.
We are dealing with dates as a subject-matter of commerce; and it is contended that, although these dates were under water for two days, and when brought up were simply a mass of pulpy matter impregnated with sewage and in a state of fermentation, there had been no change in their nature, and they still were dates. There is a perfectly well known test which has for many years been applied to such cases as the present – that test is whether, as a matter of business, the nature of the thing has been altered. The nature of a thing is not necessarily altered because the thing itself has been damaged; wheat or rice may be damaged, but may still remain the things dealt with as wheat or rice in business. But if the nature of the thing is altered, and it becomes for business purposes something else, so that it is not dealt with by business people as the thing which it originally was, the question for determination is whether the thing insured, the original article of commerce, has become a total loss. If it is so changed in its nature by the perils of the sea as to become an unmerchantable thing, which

no buyer would buy and no honest seller would sell, then there is a total loss. That test was applied in the present case by the learned judge in the Court below, who decided as a fact that the dates had been so deteriorated that they had become something which was not merchantable as dates. If that was so, there was a total loss of the dates.

Question

Suppose that, following the events in *Asfar* v. *Blundell*, the owner of the dates had sold and delivered them as 'dates' to a buyer, could the buyer sue for breach of the description warranty contained in s. 13, or the quality warranties in s. 14? In order to be entitled to bring an action for breach of the quality warranties, need the buyer have told the seller that the goods were needed for human consumption?

McCRAE v. COMMONWEALTH DISPOSAL COMMISSION (1951) 84 C.L.R. 377 (Australia)

The defendants sold an oil tanker lying wrecked on a reef for salvage. The plaintiff at considerable expense, fitted out an expedition to salvage the vessel. No oil tanker existed, though a barge did exist near the relevant position. At first instance Webb J. held the contract void for mistake on the principle of *Couturier* v. *Hastie*.[21] He awarded damages for negligence, however.

DIXON AND FULLAGAR JJ.

The position so far, then, may be summed up as follows. It was not decided in *Couturier* v. *Hastie* (1852) 8 Ex. 40 [155 E.R. 1250]; (1853) 9 Ex. 102 [156 E.R. 43]; (1856) 5 H.L.C. 673 [10 E.R. 1065] that the contract in that case was void. The question whether it was void or not did not arise. If it had arisen, as in an action by the purchaser for damages, it would have turned on the ulterior question whether the contract was subject to an implied condition precedent. Whatever might then have been held on the facts of *Couturier* v. *Hastie* (1852) 8 Ex. 40 [155 E.R. 1250]; (1853) 9 Ex. 102 [156 E.R. 43]; (1856) 5 H.L.C. 673 [10 E.R. 1065], it is impossible in this case to imply any such term. The terms of the contract and the surrounding circumstances clearly exclude any such implication. The buyers relied upon, and acted upon, the assertion of the seller that there was a tanker in existence. It is not a case in which the parties can be seen to have proceeded on the basis of a common assumption of fact so as to justify the conclusion that the correctness of the assumption was intended by both parties to be a condition precedent to the creation of contractual obligations. The officers of the Commission made an assumption, but the plaintiffs did not make an assumption in the same sense. They knew nothing except what the Commission had told them. If they had been asked, they would certainly not have said: 'Of course, if there is no tanker, there is no contract'. They would have said: 'We shall have to go and take possession of the tanker. We simply accept the Commision's assurance that there is a tanker and the Commission's promise to give us that tanker.' The only proper construction of the contract is that it included a promise by the Commission that there was a tanker in the position specified. The Commission contracted that there was a tanker there. 'The sale in this case of a ship implies a contract that the subject of the transfer did exist in the character of a ship' (*Barr* v. *Gibson* (1838) 3 M. & W., at pp. 399, 400 [150 E.R., at pp. 1200, 1201]). If, on the other hand, the case of *Couturier* v. *Hastie* (1852) 8 Ex. 40 [155 E.R. 1250]; (1853) 9 Ex. 102 [156 E.R. 43]; (1856) 5 H.L.C. 573 [10 E.R. 1065], and this case ought to be treated as cases raising a question of 'mistake', then the Commission cannot in this case rely on any mistake as avoiding the contract, because any mistake was induced by the serious fault of their own servants, who asserted the existence of a tanker recklessly and without any reasonable ground. There was a contract, and the Commission contracted that a tanker existed in the position specified. Since there was no such tanker, there has been a breach of contract, and the plaintiffs are entitled to damages for that breach.

Questions

Although on appeal the plaintiff was allowed damages for breach of contract, that was only to the extent of the plaintiff's reliance interest, i.e. the expenses incurred in the salvage expedition. Would the damages in negligence be any different?

Is there an exception to 'caveat vendor'?

If in the case of goods changing their commercial nature as in *Asfar* v. *Blundell* (above) they may be held to have perished, and the contract therefore be avoided, it could be argued that the court would then really be deciding that the goods had ceased to fall into the commercial category within which the parties exchanged their risks. That is, that the events which had occurred had taken the case outside the risk exchange contemplated by the parties. This view is capable of generating an exception to the rule 'caveat vendor'. Is it the basis of the following case?

SHERWOOD v. WALKER (1887) 33 N.W. 919 Supreme Court of Michigan

A cow, Rose 2nd of Aberlone, was thought to be barren, and was sold by her owner as meat at a price much lower than she would have fetched as a breeder. Before delivery, she was found to be with calf, and the seller refused to hand her over. The buyer sued in replevin.

MORSE J.
It appears from the record that both parties supposed this cow was

barren and would not breed, and she was sold by the pound for an insignificant sum as compared with her real value if a breeder. She was evidently sold and purchased on the relation of her value for beef, unless the plaintiff had learned of her true condition, and concealed such knowledge from the defendants. Before the plaintiff secured the possession of the animal, the defendants learned that she was with calf, and therefore of great value, and undertook to rescind the sale by refusing to deliver her. The question arises whether they had a right to do so. The circuit judge ruled that this fact did not avoid the sale and it made no difference whether she was barren or not. I am of the opinion that the court erred in this holding. I know that this is a close question, and the dividing line between the adjudicated cases is not easily discerned. But it must be considered as well settled that a party who has given an apparent consent to a contract of sale may refuse to execute it, or he may avoid it after it has been completed, if the assent was founded, or the contract made upon the mistake of a material fact, – such as the subject-matter of the sale, the price, or some collateral fact materially inducing the agreement; and this can be done when the mistake is mutual. . .

If there is a difference or misapprehension as to the substance of the thing bargained for; if the thing actually delivered or received is different in substance from the thing bargained for, and intended to be sold, – then there is no contract; but if it be only a difference in some quality or accident, even though the mistake may have been the actuating motive to the purchaser or seller, or both of them, yet the contract remains binding. 'The difficulty in every case is to determine whether the mistake or misapprehension is as to the substance of the whole contract, going, as it were, to the root of the matter, or only to some point, even though a material point, an error as to which does not affect the substance of the whole consideration.' *Kennedy* v. *Panama, etc., Mail Co.*, L.R. 2 Q.B. 580, 587. It has been held, in accordance with the principles above stated, that where a horse is bought under the belief that he is sound, and both vendor and vendee honestly believe him to be sound, the purchaser must stand by his bargain, and pay the full price, unless there was a warranty.

It seems to me, however, in the case made by this record, that the mistake or misapprehension of the parties went to the whole substance of the agreement. If the cow was a breeder, she was worth at least $750; if barren, she was worth not over $80. The parties would not have made the contract of sale except upon the understanding and belief that she was incapable of breeding, and of no use as a cow. It is true she is now the identical animal that they thought her to be when the contract was made; there is no mistake as to the identity of the creature. Yet the mistake was not of the mere quality of the animal, but went to the very nature of the thing. A barren cow is substantially a different creature than a breeding one. There is as much difference between them for all purposes of use as there is between an ox and a cow that is capable of breeding, and giving milk. If the mutual mistake had simply related to the fact whether she was with calf or not for one season, then it might have been a good sale, but the mistake affected the character of the animal for all time, and for its present and ultimate use. She was not in fact the animal, or the kind of animal, the defendants intended to sell or the plaintiff to buy. She was not a barren cow, and, if this fact had been known, there would have been no contract. The mistake affected the substance of the whole consideration, and it must be considered that there was no contract to sell or sale of the cow as she actually was. The thing sold and bought had in fact no existence. She was sold as a beef creature would be sold; she is in fact a breeding cow, and a valuable one. The Court should have instructed the jury that if they found that the cow was sold, or contracted to be sold, upon the understanding of both parties that she was barren, and useless for the purpose of breeding, and that in fact she was not barren, but capable of breeding, then the defendants had a right to rescind, and to refuse to deliver, and the verdict should be in their favour.

Campbell C.J. and Champlin J. concurred, Sherwood J. dissented.

Note

In *Wood* v. *Boynton*[22] (1885) 25 N.W. 42 a girl sold a stone the size of a canary's egg to a jeweller for $1. It was a diamond worth $700. The contract was held to be valid. Can you reconcile this case with *Sherwood* v. *Walker*? Where such mistakes are made by the *buyer*, the situation is regulated by the quality warranty provisions of the Sale of Goods Act. There would seem to be no need for a doctrine of mistake therefore. See, however, *Nicholson and Venn* v. *Smith Marriott*.[23]

The effect of express agreement

It was suggested above that in avoiding a contract for the sale of specific goods which perish without fault on the part of the seller before the risk has passed to the buyer, the Act in effect makes a policy decision: the loss which has occurred has gone beyond the exchange of risks forming the subject-matter of the contract. It is, however, open to the parties expressly to provide for this by stipulating the circumstances in which the seller's duty to deliver the goods will terminate. This duty can in theory be stricter than the Act's – the seller can theoretically enter into an absolute obligation to deliver (as Holmes pointed out in *The Common Law*, you can contract that it will rain if you like[24]), in which case the seller would become, as it were, the insurer of the buyer's interest. More probably the parties will wish to stipulate more extensive avoidance provisions than the Act's, which are limited to *specific* goods which *perish*. A common clause found in commercial contracts protects the seller in the event of non-delivery being due to *force majeur*, a somewhat uncertain term derived from the *Code Napoléon*, but which at least indicates something less than an act of God. Acts of sovereign states which prevent the delivery of the goods are clear examples of *force majeur*. The following case illustrates this.

C. CZARNIKOW LTD v. CENTRALA HANDLU ZAGRANICZNEGO ROLIMPEX [1978] 1 Q.B. 176

Rolimpex, a Polish state enterprise, sold 200,000 tonnes of sugar to the plaintiffs. The Rules of the Refined Sugar Association were incorporated into the contract. Rule 18 contained a *force majeur* provision to the effect that if delivery was prevented, *inter alia*, by 'government intervention . . . beyond the seller's control' the contract would be void without penalty. Rule 21 made Rolimpex responsible for obtaining an export licence. They failed to obtain this because of an export ban imposed by the Polish government. The Court of Appeal held 2:1 that the contract was frustrated. All the judges reached their decisions on the basis that Rolimpex was a separate entity from the Polish state.

LORD DENNING M.R.

In this case there is an express term, not an implied term: so the problem here is one of construction. Was the duty of the seller (to obtain a licence) an absolute duty to obtain one or pay damages? Or was it only a duty to use reasonable diligence to obtain a licence?

Now take this rule 21 and read the first few lines of it. It says:

> The buyer shall be responsible for obtaining any necessary import licence and the seller shall be responsible for obtaining any necessary export licence. The failure to obtain such licence shall not be sufficient grounds for a claim of *force majeur*. . .

Stopping there, it is plain that it applies to all cases where, at the time of contract, an export licence is necessary. Even though the seller used all diligence to obtain a licence and nevertheless it was refused, he would be liable in damages to the buyer. He could not avail himself of any excuse, not even of *force majeur*. So his responsibility, to obtain an export licence, would be an absolute responsibility, not a restricted one. Then go to the succeedings words: '. . . if the regulations in force at the time when the contract was made, called for such licences to be obtained.' Those words are inserted so as to aid a seller who finds himself in this position: At the time of the contract, an export licence was not necessary. The regulations then in force did not call for an export licence, but then, after the contract, new regulations are made calling for an export licence. In that situation, it is only fair that a seller should *not* then be absolutely liable to obtain an export licence. If he uses reasonable diligence and fails to obtain one – so that it would be illegal for him to export – then it would be 'a cause of *force majeur* beyond the seller's control' excepting him under Rule 18(a). Per contra, when the regulations in force at the time of the contract call for a licence to be obtained, his duty is absolute. He must obtain the licence or pay damages.

Now in the present case at the time of the contract an export licence was necessary: and the sellers did in fact obtain the necessary export licence. So they did fulfil their obligation under Rule 21, absolute as it was. They had done all that the contract required of them.

But then, on top of it all, just at the very last point – as the goods were about to be shipped – the Government of Poland imposed a ban on all exports of sugar. What was the duty of the sellers in that situation? Did Rule 21 require them at that stage to obtain 'any necessary export licence'? I cannot think so. The rule was not applicable in this new situation. No licences were obtainable at all. The ban was absolute. It would be ridiculous to expect the sellers to apply for an export licence. I cannot think they should be made liable in that situation – when there was absolutely nothing they could do. They had done everything that the contract required them to do. It was only the ban – that is, the government intervention – which prevented the shipment. It was a clear case of *force majeur*. They were excused from liability for it by rule 18(a).

Sales in a string

In c.i.f. contracts (q.v.) the seller usually has the option either to ship goods or to purchase goods afloat. What happens if the original sale is followed by a string of sub-sales, and, as in *Czarnikow* v. *Rolimpex* (above), the original contract is frustrated by an export ban? Will the theoretical possibility of the sellers buying afloat prevent them from arguing that the contract is frustrated? The answer is 'no'. The reason for this is explained by Lord Denning M.R. in the following passage:

TRADEX EXPORT S.A. v. ANDRE & CIE S.A. [1976] 1 Ll. Rep. 416

LORD DENNING M.R.

Take the usual case of a string of contracts between the shipper and the receiver. If there were an obligation to buy afloat, who is to do the buying? Is each seller to do so in order to fulfil his obligation to the buyer? If that were so there would be . . . large numbers of buyers chasing very few goods and the price would reach unheard of levels. Alternatively, is the first seller in the string to do so? Or the last seller? No one can tell. It seems to me that if there is prohibition of export or *force majeur*, the sellers are bound to buy afloat in order to implement their contract.

3 When Does the Risk Pass to the Buyer?

(1) THE *PRIMA FACIE* RULE

The subject-matter of a contract for the sale of goods is not in law the transfer of possession of goods, but the transfer of property in goods (s. 2. Sale of Goods Act). It follows that if the property has passed to the buyer, he must pay the price if the goods are damaged or destroyed without fault on the part of the seller, even though he has never had possession nor even been entitled to it.[25] This is an exceedingly unsatisfactory rule, since in many cases it is difficult to say when property has passed. A much simpler rule would be to place the risk on the party in possession, so that it passes when possession is transferred from the seller to the buyer:

Bracton: DE LEGIBUS (c. 1250) (Thorne ed. Vol. II p. 183)

Once a purchase and sale has been concluded, as was said above, the risk attending the thing bought and sold, both before delivery and after it, fall generally upon him who has it in his possession, unless it is otherwise agreed at the outset, for obviously he who has not yet delivered the thing to its buyer will still himself be its owner, since by deliveries and usucapions etc. as above in the portion on gifts may readily be seen, as where a slave sold dies before delivery, or a house is consumed by fire, or an estate is wholly or partially wasted or swept away by the force of a stream and the like, for which reasons it seems that the whole risk falls upon the seller.

The Uniform Commercial Code has abandoned the arbitrary shifting of risk with property rule, in favour of a risk with possession rule.[26] Our rule suffers from two serious defects: (1) it creates a high degree of uncertainty in an area where certainty is crucially important; (2) it is quite likely to place the loss on the party least likely to be insured against it. By contrast, a transfer of risk with delivery rule is both clear and calculated to place the loss where the insurance lies.

It is important to bear in mind, however, that the rules are merely *prima facie*. The parties can clarify the matter by stipulating themselves when the risk is to pass. Furthermore, many mercantile contracts will in practice take place under the code letters f.o.b., c.i.f., f.a.s., etc.

DOI: 10.4324/9781003174615-4

These terms are internationally used and, amongst other things, imply clear rules for the passing of the risk (see pp. 42 et seq., below).

UNDERWOOD v. BURGH CASTLE BRICK AND CEMENT SYNDICATE [1922] 1 K.B. 343

The subject-matter of the sale in this case was a condensing engine which at the time of the contract was bolted to, and embedded in, a flooring of concrete. In order that it could be delivered, it had to be detached and dismantled. The sellers duly detached it, but damaged it by accident while loading it into a railway truck. The buyers refused to accept delivery.[27] The issue was therefore whether or not the property, and therefore the risk, had passed to the buyer at the time the damage occurred.

BANKES L.J.

Did the property in that engine pass on the contract of sale? No general rule can be laid down which will answer the question when the property passes in every contract of sale. In many sales of specific articles to be delivered the property passes on the making of the contract. A man may select and agree to buy a hat and the shopman may agree to deliver it at the buyer's house. There notwithstanding the obligation to deliver the hat, the property passes at the time of the contract. But that is far from this case. Considering the risk and expense involved in dismantling and moving this engine, I have no hesitation in holding that the proper inference to be drawn is that the property was not to pass until the engine was safely placed on rail in London. In my view an elaborate discussion of the rules in s. 18 of the Sale of Goods Act, 1893 is unnecessary. They only apply where a different intention does not appear, and in this case a different intention does appear, assuming for the moment that this machine was in a deliverable state when it was fixed in its position at Millwall. In *Badische Anilin und Soda Fabrik* v. *Basle Chemical Works* [1898] A.C. 200, 207 Lord Herschell put a hypothetical case in which the facts would lead to the same inference – namely, of an intention different from the effect of s. 18, r. 1. But was this engine in a deliverable state in its position at Millwall? The appellants contended that where a specific article is complete in itself, for example a complete engine or a complete cart – that is to say, where nothing more has to be done to make it an engine or a cart – it is then in a deliverable state within the meaning of s. 18, r. 1., and if the owner agrees to sell it the property passes to the buyer when the contract is made, and it is immaterial whether the time of payment or the time of delivery, or both, be postponed. I do not accept that test. A 'deliverable state' does not depend upon the mere completeness of the subject matter in all its parts. It depends on the actual state of the goods at the date of the contract and the state in which they are to be delivered by the terms of the contract. Where the vendors have to expend as much trouble and as much money as the appellants had to expend before this engine could be placed on rail, I cannot think that the subject matter can be said to be in a deliverable state. The appeal must be dismissed.

Note

The contract in this case contained the term 'f.o.b. London'. An alternative ground for the decision might have been that this implied that the risk passed only when the goods were loaded into the truck (see pp. 42 et seq., below).

Questions

1. This engine was fixed to land, since what is fixed to land is part of the land, how could this be a contract for the sale of goods?
2. At first instance, Rowlatt J. suggested that the mere fact that a chattel, such as a sideboard, needs to be dismantled before delivery, does not prevent the passing of property. Can you reconcile this with the Court of Appeal decision?

CARLOS FEDERSPIEL AND CO. v. CHARLES TWIGG [1957] 1 Ll. Rep. 240

The defendants contracted to sell cycles to the plaintiffs f.o.b. British port. The defendants duly manufactured the cycles, and packed them in containers with the plaintiff's name and address on them. Before shipment, however, the defendants became insolvent. If the property had passed to the plaintiffs, they were entitled to the goods *vis-à-vis* the defendants' receiver.

PEARSON J.
On those authorities, what are the principles emerging? I think one can distinguish these principles. First, Rule 5 of Sect. 18 of the Act is one of the Rules for ascertaining the intention of the parties as to the time at which the property in the goods is to pass to the buyer unless a different intention appears. Therefore the element of common intention has always to be borne in mind. A mere setting apart or selection of the seller of the goods which he expects to use in performance of the contract is not enough. If that is all, he can change his mind and use those goods in performance of some other contract and use some other goods in performance of this contract. To constitute an appropriation of the goods to the contract, the parties must have had, or be reasonably supposed to have had, an intention to attach the contract irrevocably to those goods, so that those goods and no others are the subject of the sale and become the property of the buyer.

Secondly, it is by agreement of the parties that the appropriation, involving a change of ownership, is made, although in some cases the buyer's assent to an appropriation by the seller is conferred in advance by the contract itself or otherwise.

Thirdly, an appropriation by the seller, with the assent of the buyer, may be said always to involve an actual or constructive delivery. If the seller retains possession, he does so as bailee for the buyer. There is a passage in Chalmers' *Sale of Goods Act*, 12th ed., at p. 75, where it is said:

> In the second place, if the decisions be carefully examined, it will be found that in every case where the property has been held to pass, there has been an actual or constructive delivery of the goods to the buyer.

I think that is right, subject only to this possible qualification, that there may be after such constructive delivery an actual delivery still to be made by the seller under the contract. Of course, that is quite possible, because delivery is the transfer of possession, whereas appropriation transfers ownership. So there may be first an appropriation, constructive delivery, whereby the seller becomes bailee for the buyer, and then a subsequent actual delivery involving actual possession, and when I say that I have in mind in particular the two cases cited, namely, *Aldridge* v. *Johnson* (1857) 7 E. & B. 885, and *Langton* v. *Higgins* (1859) 4 H. & N. 402.

Fourthly, one has to remember Sect. 20 of the Sale of Goods Act, whereby the ownership and the risk are normally associated. Therefore as it appears that there is reason for thinking, on the construction of the relevant documents, that the goods were, at all material times, still at the seller's risk, that is *prima facie* an indication that the property had not passed to the buyer.

Fifthly, usually but not necessarily, the appropriating act is the last act to be performed by the seller. For instance, if delivery is to be taken by the buyer at the seller's premises and the seller has completed his part of the contract and has appropriated the goods when he has made the goods ready and has identified them and placed them in position to be taken by the buyer and has so informed the buyer, and if the buyer agrees to come and take them, that is the assent to the appropriation. But if there is a further act, an important and decisive act to be done by the seller, then there is *prima facie* evidence that probably the property does not pass until the final act is done.

Applying those principles to the present case I would say this. Firstly, the intention was that the ownership should pass on shipment (or possibly at some later date) because the emphasis is throughout on shipment as the decisive act to be done by the seller in performance of the contract. Secondly, it is impossible to find in this correspondence an agreement to a change of ownership before the time of shipment. The letters, especially those of Aug. 27 and Sept. 14, which are particularly relied on by the plaintiff, do not contain any provision or implication of any earlier change of ownership. Thirdly, there is no actual or constructive delivery; no suggestion of the seller becoming a bailee for the buyer. Fourthly, there is no suggestion of the goods being at the buyer's risk at any time before shipment; no suggestion that the buyer should insist on the seller arranging insurance for them. Fifthly, the last two acts to be performed by the seller, namely, sending the goods to Liverpool and having the goods shipped on board, were not performed.

Therefore, my decision that the *prima facie* inference which one would have drawn from the contract is that the property was not to pass at any time before shipment, is in my view not displaced by the subsequent correspondence between the parties. It follows, therefore, that there was no appropriation of these goods and therefore the action fails.

Question

Pearson J. seems to have considered it material that risk would not pass before shipment: indeed this would generally be the case in an f.o.b. contract. Does it necessarily follow from this that property would only pass on shipment?

(2) DISPLACEMENT OF THE *PRIMA FACIE* RULE

(a) Risk passing to buyer before property has passed

STERNS v. VICKERS [1923] 1 K.B. 78

The defendants sold 120,000 gallons of white spirit to the plaintiffs. The spirit was part of a larger quantity of spirit stored in a tank. The plaintiffs were given a delivery warrant enabling them to obtain possession at any time. However, before the plaintiffs took delivery the spirit in the tank deteriorated.

SCRUTTON L.J.
I think Mr Thorn Drury is right in saying that as at the material time there had been no severance of the quantity purchased from the larger bulk there were no specific 120,000 gallons in which the property passed. The question as to the effect of such a sale of an undivided portion of a larger bulk has frequently arisen in the Courts, and was much discussed in the well-known case of *Inglis* v. *Stock* (1885) 10 App. Cas. 263, where a similar argument to that which was addressed to us here was addressed to the Court for the purpose of showing that a person who had bought a certain number of tons of sugar, part of a larger stock, had no insurable interest in the quantity bought, because no specific bags had been appropriated to the contract and consequently the property in them had not passed. But as Lord Blackburn there pointed out, although the purchaser did not acquire the property in any particular number of tons of sugar he did acquire an undivided interest in the larger bulk and that undivided interest the House of Lords held to be insurable. The acquisition of an undivided interest in a larger bulk clearly will not suffice to pass

the property when the appropriation to the contract has to be made by the vendor himself. As Bayley B. said in *Gillett* v. *Hill* (1834) 2 Cr. & M. 530, 535: 'Where there is a bargain for a certain quantity' of goods 'ex a great quantity, and there is a power of selection in the vendor to delivery which he thinks fit, then the right to them does not pass to the vendee until the vendor has made his selection, and trover is not maintainable before that is done.' Nor probably will the acquisition of such an undivided interest pass the property, so as to entitle the purchaser to sue for a conversion, in a case where the power of appropriation is, as here, in a third party. But in that latter case, whether the property passes or not, the transfer of the undivided interest carries with it the risk of loss from something happening to the goods, such as a deterioration in their quality, at all events after the vendor has given the purchaser a delivery order upon the party in possession of them, and that party has assented to it. The vendor of a specified quantity out of a bulk in the possession of a third party discharges his obligation to the purchaser as soon as the third party undertakes to the purchaser to deliver him that quantity out of the bulk. In the present case, what happened was that at the date of the contract there was a bulk larger than the quantity sold, and it was of the contract quality according to sample. A delivery warrant was issued by the Thames Haven Company undertaking to deliver that quantity from the bulk which at that time corresponded with the sample. That warrant was accepted by the purchaser and by their sub-purchaser, Lazarus, who proceeded to pay rent for the storage from the date of the warrant. In those circumstances I come clearly to the conclusion that as between the plaintiffs and the defendants the risk was on the plaintiffs the purchasers. The vendors had done all that they undertook to do. The purchasers had the right to go to the storage company and demand delivery, and if they had done so at the time they would have got all that the defendants had undertaken to sell them. What the purchasers here are trying to do is to put the risk after acceptance of the warrant upon persons who had then no control over the goods, for it seems plain that after the acceptance of that warrant the vendors would have had no right to go to the storage company and request them to refuse delivery to the purchaser. For these reasons, treating the matter as a question rather of the transfer of risk than of the passing of property – for strictly I do not think the property passed, but only a right to an undivided share in the bulk to be selected by a third person – I think the view taken by the judge below was erroneous. He seems to have considered the question of transferring the risk, and thought there was no evidence of it. With that view I cannot agree. I think the only conclusion to be drawn from the evidence is that the risk did pass. The appeal must be allowed.

Questions

1. Is it a material that the subject-matter of the contract was part of a quantity of liquid in a tank which by its nature deteriorates

in its entirety?

2. What would be the position, on otherwise identical facts, if the contract involved the sale of 200 bags of sugar out of a bulk of 400 bags, but only 300 bags had deteriorated? – see the two following cases.

INGLIS v. STOCK (1885) 10 A.C. 263

Drake and Co. sold Beloe 200 tons of sugar f.o.b. Hamburg. They also sold a further 200 tons to Stock. 390 tons (i.e. 10 tons short) were shipped in fulfilment of these contracts. The vessel sank, and the sugar was lost. Drake then allocated 200 tons to Beloe's contract.

LORD BLACKBURN

When Drake & Co., or rather their agents at Hamburg, were shipping the sugar and held the mate's notes, it was no doubt their business to see that a proper bill of lading for each separate shipment was signed; and if at any time before the bills of lading left Hamburg they had been allocated to each shipment, no objection, not even an idle one, could have been raised. But instead of doing so the whole of the bills were sent in a lump to London that they might be allocated there. This was perfectly bona fide. Drake & Co. had no interest in favouring one more than the other, and were to be paid exactly the same price per bag, whether they allocated it to the one or to the other. And if they had done this before the loss, I do not see what damage either Beloe or Stock could have sustained by the allocation being made in London instead of in Hamburg.

Now I have been quite unable to see, even if the plaintiff had sustained some damage, that it could have been damage going to the whole root of the matter, so as to form a defence for the plaintiff against an action by either Drake & Co. or Beloe for not paying for the goods in exchange for the bills of lading; that is, supposing the plaintiff (because prices had greatly fallen, or from any other unworthy motive) had wished to get off.

And if it were so, I think the case would fall entirely within what Lord Hatherley, in *Anderson* v. *Morice* 1 App. Cas. 735, says is the principle of *Sparkes* v. *Marshall* 2 Bing. N.C. 761. The insurers have no right to call upon the insured to exercise a possible option to be released from their contract. But the loss having happened before the actual allocation, the plaintiff's loss, when it happened, was a loss not of 200 tons, but of 200 tons parcel of 390 tons, so that the loss, though exactly the same, is said not to be the same in description, because it is the loss of an undivided portion of the goods, instead of being the loss of the goods themselves. I am quite unable myself to perceive why that should make the slightest difference. In the merits, certainly it does not. I am quite unable to perceive why an undivided interest in a parcel of goods on board a ship may not be described as an interest in goods just as much as if it were an interest in every portion of the goods. No authority was cited in order to shew that it was not so, and I can see no reason for it. Then, that being so, of course it follows that there is no defence at all, and this is my opinion.

HEALY v. HOWLETT [1917] 1 K.B. 337

The plaintiff sold twenty boxes of mackerel to the defendant. He dispatched 190 boxes, twenty boxes for the defendant and the remaining 170 boxes for two other consignees. None of the boxes was earmarked for a specific consignee. The mackerel deteriorated in transit. On arrival, twenty boxes were appropriated to the defendant's contract. The defendant rejected.

RIDLEY J.
I am not aware that in any similar case it has been held that because all the parcels were meant to be divided between three separate purchasers in London there was an appropriation of them all to the risk of the purchasers when it was impossible to say at whose risk any one of the boxes could be. It would follow in the present case that if there was delivery or appropriation, as the learned judge in the Court below put it, up to a certain point, although not completely, at Valentia, some process of lottery or allotment would have to be adopted to decide upon which consignee the loss was to fall if a portion of the goods disappeared and the other portion did not. It is difficult to understand how that could possibly be done. Supposing half the boxes had been lost at sea and the other half were safe, it would be impossible to say whether the boxes which had been lost were the property of the defendants or of one of the other two consignees. In order to bring the present case within the authorities as to appropriation passing the property each box ought to have been marked with the name of its consignee. From that moment the boxes would have remained at the risk of the consignees respectively. That seems to me to be the principle laid down in the Sale of Goods Act, 1893, so far as that statute in terms deals with the matter.

Questions

1. Can you reconcile this decision with *Inglis* v. *Stock*?
2. Was it a material fact that the contract in *Inglis* v. *Stock* contained an f.o.b. term? See pp 42 et seq., below.

(b) Risk remaining with seller after passing of property

HEAD v. TATTERSALL (1870) L.R. 7 Ex. 7

The plaintiff bought a horse warranted hunted with the Bicester. It was provided that he might return it up to the following Wednesday if it did not answer to its description. The plaintiff discovered that it had not been hunted with the Bicester. He returned the horse within the time allowed, but it had been injured without his fault while in his possession. Was he entitled to recover the price?

BRAMWELL B.
. . . it is said the right to return was lost, because the rule is that a buyer cannot return a specific chattel except it be in the same state as when it was bought. That is quite true as a general proposition, but in such a case as the present the rule must, in my opinion, be qualified thus:— The buyer must return the horse in the same condition as when he bought it, but subject to any of those incidents to which the horse may be liable, either from its inherent nature, or in the course of the exercise by the buyer of those rights over it which the contract gave. For example, suppose the horse, while standing in the stable, strained itself or injured a limb, that would not affect the right of return, although the horse would no longer be exactly in the same condition as before. So here, where, without the plaintiff's default, but while he was doing with the horse what he had a right to do under his contract, the horse was injured, I do not think the right to return it was lost.

Problem

B ordered some shirts by mail order. The contract provided that the goods might be returned in seven days if he was not satisfied. The shirts were unmerchantable. Unfortunately, before he could return them in the time allocated, they were completely destroyed through no fault of his. Can he reclaim the price? (See P. Atiyah, *Sale of Goods*, 6th ed., p. 205.)

(c) The effect of default by either party[28]

DENBY HAMILTON & CO. v. BARDEN [1949] 1 All E.R. 435

The plaintiff contracted to sell 30 tons of apple juice to the defendant. Apples were duly crushed, and put ready for collection. The buyer collected only 20½ tons. The remainder went putrid because of the buyer's delay.

SELLERS J.
The first requirement of the proviso in question is that delivery has been delayed through the fault of the buyer. I am satisfied on the facts in the present case that a good delivery, which would have avoided all loss, was delayed through the fault of the buyer. . . The next requirement of the proviso is that, where delivery has been delayed through the fault of the buyer, the goods are at the risk of the party in fault 'as regards any loss which might not have occurred but for such fault.' The goods referred to there must be the contractual goods which have been assembled by the seller for the purpose of fulfilling his contract and making delivery. The goods may have been defined goods, goods

manufactured for the purposes of delivery, or goods which had been acquired by the seller from somebody else for the purpose of fulfilling his contract. It does not seem to me that the Act requires to be construed in any narrow sense. The real question is whether the loss which has accrued was brought about by the delay in delivery, and that must have regard to the goods which were there to be delivered. Different circumstances may arise in different cases. It may be that the seller was in a position to sell the goods elsewhere and acquire other goods for the postponed time of delivery, and if he does not do that and there is some loss in the meantime the responsibility for the loss would be held to fall upon him. Again, there may be cases (and I think this is one of them) where the seller has his goods ready for delivery and has to keep them ready for delivery as and when the buyer proposes to take them. In the present case the position is clear. The casks of apple juice which were not accepted were manufactured at the time of the contract, and the contract required that delivery should be in accordance with sample. It would have been very difficult to have obtained goods which complied with the sample unless the apples had all been crushed at the same time. They would have had to be apples from the same district and the juice from them, when obtained, would have had to be of the same maturity. The condition of apples changes. They may be unripe at one time and too ripe at another. The 30 tons of juice were goods which the sellers rightly and reasonably kept for the fulfilment of their contract. These were the last apples which the sellers had that season for crushing, and, therefore, the goods in question were goods which the sellers had awaiting delivery in fulfilment of their contract with the buyer.

I have to ask myself whether this loss might not have occurred but for the fault of the buyer. I am satisfied that it would not have occurred but for his fault. There is, of course, an obligation on a seller to act reasonably, and, if possible, to avoid any loss. As to that, one or two questions arise for consideration. Was there anything the seller could reasonably do to dispose of these goods when they still had an outstanding obligation to keep them at the disposal of the buyer and when they had to be ready and willing to deliver them when requested? If delivery had been asked for at a later date and they had let these goods go elsewhere they could not have fulfilled their contract. I do not hesitate to find (although to construe this proviso is not easy) that in a practical and business sense this loss has fallen on the sellers by reason of the fact that the buyer refused to take delivery at the proper time and postponed the date of delivery until the goods had deteriorated, and I come to the conclusion that the liability for that loss falls on the buyer.

Note

It is not clear from the report of this case why the property had not passed under s. 18, r. 5(1), Sale of Goods Act, it is clearly distinguishable from *Carlos Federspiel* v. *Charles Twigg* (above).

(3) F.O.B. AND C.I.F. CONTRACTS

These terms are not defined in the Sale of Goods Act although s. 32 does have bearing on them. The Uniform Commercial Code (1978 text) defines them as follows:

2-319

(1) Unless otherwise agreed the term f.o.b. (which means 'free on board') at a named place, even though used only in connection with the stated price, is a delivery term under which:

(a) When the term is f.o.b. the place of shipment, the seller must at that place ship the goods in the manner provided in this Article (Section 2-504) and bear the expense and risk of putting them into the possession of the carrier; or

(b) When the term is f.o.b. the place of destination, the seller must at his own expense and risk transport the goods to that place and there tender delivery of them in the manner provided in this Article (Section 2-503);

(c) When under either (a) or (b) the term is also f.o.b. vessel, car or other vehicle, the seller must in addition at his own expense and risk load the goods on board. If the term is f.o.b. vessel the buyer must name the vessel and in an appropriate case the seller must comply with the provisions of this Article on the form of bill of lading (Section 2-323).

2-320

(1) The term c.i.f. means that the price includes in a lump sum the cost of the goods and the insurance and freight to the named destination. The term c. & f. or c.f. means that the price so includes cost and freight to the named destination.

(2) Unless otherwise agreed and even though used only in connection with the stated price and destination, the term c.i.f. destination or its equivalent requires the seller at his own expense and risk to

(a) Put the goods into the possession of a carrier at the port for shipment and obtain a negotiable bill or bills of lading covering the entire transportation to the named destination; and

(b) Load the goods and obtain a receipt from the carrier (which may be contained in the bill of lading) showing that the freight has been paid or provided for; and

(c) Obtain a policy or certificate of insurance, including any war-risk insurance, of a kind and on terms then current at the port of shipment in the usual amount, in the currency of the contract, shown to cover the same goods covered by the bill of lading and providing for payment of loss to the order of the buyer or for the account of whom it may concern; but the seller may add to the price the amount of the premium for any such war-risk insurance; and

(d) Prepare an invoice of the goods and procure any other documents required to effect shipment or to comply with the contract; and

(e) Forward and tender with commercial promptness all the documents in due form and with any indorsement necessary to perfect the buyer's rights.

(3) Unless otherwise agreed the term c. & f. or its equivalent has the same effect and imposes upon the seller the same obligations and risks as a c.i.f. term except the obligation as to insurance.

(4) Under the term c.i.f. or c. & f. unless otherwise agreed the buyer must make payment against tender of the required documents and the seller may not tender nor the buyer demand delivery of the goods in substitution for the documents.

Note

In the United Kingdom and Commonwealth f.o.b. is understood *inter alia* to require the seller to place the goods on board a ship.[29] It will be appreciated that under American practice reflected by 2-319, 'f.o.b.' has become a general delivery term, thus 'f.o.b. place of destination'. Subject to this, 2-319 and 2-320 could provide a useful model if it were thought desirable to enact legislation in this country. As it is, f.o.b. and c.i.f. contracts depend principally for their effect on the common law and commercial custom in this country. For both categories of contract a clearer and more commercially workable set of principles governing the risk of loss or damage to the goods apply than in sales of goods governed purely by the general risk passing with property rule.

In the case of f.o.b. contracts the general rule is that risk passes when the goods pass over the ship's rail. The buyer should have insurance cover from that point. In the case of c.i.f. contracts, the seller usually has the option either to ship goods, or to buy afloat. His duty is to deliver the documents, i.e. the bill of lading and certificate of insurance to the buyer, not physically to deliver the goods themselves. The buyer must pay against the tender of the documents and cannot complain that up to that time he has had no opportunity to examine the goods, nor even that they are known to have perished. Of course, when the goods are finally physically delivered, the buyer has the normal right to reject for a non-conformity amounting to a breach of condition (s. 11(3)) until he is deemed to have accepted them (ss. 34 and 35). If the non-conformity is due to damage during the voyage, he has no right to reject, of course, because that damage should be covered by the insurance policy transferred to him by the seller.

E. CLEMENS HORST CO. v. BIDDELL BROS [1912] A.C. 18

Horst sold hops to V 'c.i.f. to London, Liverpool or Hull'. V assigned their rights to Biddells. Biddells refused to pay for the hops before delivery and examination. It was held that the seller was entitled to payment on shipment of the goods and tender of the bill of lading and insurance policy. Kennedy L.J.'s dissenting judgement [1911] 1 K.B. 934, 952 was approved by the House of Lords.

KENNEDY L.J.

The application of the principles and rules of the common law, now embodied in the Sale of Goods Act, 1893, to the business transaction embodied in the c.i.f. contract appears to me to be decisive of the issue between these parties. Let us see, step by step, how according to those principles and rules the transaction specified in such a c.i.f. contract as that before us is and, I think, must be carried out in order to fulfil its terms.

At the port of shipment – in this case San Francisco – the vendor ships the goods intended for the purchaser under the contract. Under the Sale of Goods Act, 1893, s. 18, by such shipment the goods are appropriated by the vendor to the fulfilment of the contract, and by virtue of s. 32 the delivery of the goods to the carrier – whether named by the purchaser or not – for the purpose of transmission to the purchaser is *prima facie* to be deemed to be a delivery of the goods to the purchaser. Two further legal results arise out of the shipment. The goods are at the risk of the purchaser, against which he has protected himself by the stipulation in his c.i.f. contract that the vendor shall, at his own cost, provide him with a proper policy of marine insurance intended to protect the buyer's interest, and available for his use, if the goods should be lost in transit; and the property in the goods has passed to the purchaser, either conditionally or unconditionally. It passes conditionally where the bill of lading for the goods, for the purpose of better securing payment of the price, is made out in favour of the vendor or his agent or representative: see the judgements of Bramwell L.J. and Cotton L.J. in *Mirabita* v. *Imperial Ottoman Bank* ((1878) 3 Ex. D. 164). It passes unconditionally where the bill of lading is made out in favour of the purchaser or his agent or representative, as consignee. But the vendor, in absence of special agreement, is not yet in a position to demand payment from the purchaser; his delivery of the goods to the carrier is, according to the express terms of s. 32 only '*prima facie* deemed to be a delivery of the goods to the buyer'; and under s. 28 of the Sale of Goods Act, as under the common law (an exposition of which will be found in the judgements of the members of the Exchequer Chamber in the old case of *Startup* v. *Macdonald* 6 Man. & G. 593), a tender of delivery entitling the vendor to payment of the price must, in the absence of contractual stipulation to the contrary, be a tender of possession. How is such a tender to be made of goods afloat under a c.i.f. contract? By tender of the bill of lading, accompanied in case the goods have been lost in transit by the policy of insurance. The bill of lading in law and in fact represents the goods. Possession of the bill of lading places the goods at the disposal of the purchaser. A 'cargo at sea,' says Bowen L.J. in *Sanders* v. *Maclean* 11 Q.B.D. 327, 341, 'while in the hands of the carrier, is necessarily incapable of physical delivery. During this period of transit and voyage, the bill of lading by the law merchant is universally recognized as its symbol, and the indorsement and delivery of the bill of lading operates as a symbolical delivery of the cargo. Property in the goods passes by such indorsement and delivery of the bill of lading, whenever it is the intention of the parties that the property should pass, just as under similar circumstances the property would pass by an actual delivery of the goods. And for the purpose of passing such property in the goods and completing the title of the indorsee to full possession thereof, the bill of lading, until complete delivery of the cargo has been made on shore to some one rightfully claiming under it, remains in force as a symbol, and carries with it not only the full ownership of the goods but also all rights created by the contract of carriage between the shipper and the shipowner. It is a key which in the hands of a rightful owner is intended to unlock the door of the warehouse, floating or fixed, in which the goods may chance to be.' The meaning of 'delivery' under the Sale of Goods Act is defined by s. 62 to be 'voluntary transfer of possession from one person to another.' Such delivery, as the learned draftsman of the Act and its editor remarks in his note to this section, may be either actual or constructive: see Chalmers' *Sale of Goods Act*, 1893, 7th ed. p. 140; and, as Bowen L.J. has pronounced, in the case of seaborne goods, the delivery of the bill of lading operates as a symbolical delivery of goods. But then I understand it to be objected on behalf of the plaintiffs: 'Granted that the purchaser might, if he pleased, take this constructive delivery and pay against it the price of the goods; what is there in the "cost freight and insurance" contract which compels him to do so? Why may he not insist on an option of waiting for a tender of delivery of the goods themselves after having had an opportunity of examining them after their arrival?'

There are, I think, sufficient answers to such a proposition. In the first place, an option of a time of payment is not a term which can be inferred, where the contract itself is silent. So far as I am aware, there is no authority for the inference of an option as to times of payment to be found either in the law books or in the Sale of Goods Act. Secondly, if there is a duty on the vendor to tender the bill of lading, there must, it seems to me, be a corresponding duty on the part of the purchaser to pay when such tender is made.

Note

If the plaintiffs' contention had been correct, the rule set out in the following case would be wrong – the purchaser could never exercise his right of examination over goods which had perished.

MANBRE SACCHARINE CO. LTD v. CORN PRODUCTS CO. LTD [1919] 1 K.B. 198

McCARDIE J.

The first question arising can be briefly stated as follows: Can a vendor under an ordinary c.i.f. contract effectively tender appropriate documents to the buyer in respect of goods shipped on a vessel which at the time of tender the vendor knows to have been totally lost? . . . I conceive that the essential feature of an ordinary c.i.f. contract as compared with an ordinary contract for the sale of goods rests in the fact that performance of the bargain is to be fulfilled by delivery of documents and not by the actual physical delivery of goods by the vendor. All that the buyer can call for is delivery of the customary documents. This represents the measure of the buyer's right and the extent of the vendor's duty. The buyer cannot refuse the documents and ask for the actual goods, nor can the vendor withhold the documents and tender the goods they represent. The position is stated with weight and clearness in the treaties on charter-parties by Scrutton L.J., 8th ed., p. 167, in the notes to article 59 as follows: 'The best way of approaching the consideration of all questions on c.i.f. sales is to realise that this form of the sale of goods is one to be performed by the delivery of documents representing the goods – i.e. of documents giving the right to have the goods delivered or the possible right, if they are lost or damaged, of recovering their value from the shipowner or from underwriters. It results from this that various rules in the Sale of Goods Act, 1893, which is primarily drafted in relation to the sale and delivery of goods on land, can only be applied to c.i.f. sales *mutatis mutandis*. And there may be cases in which the buyer must pay the full price for delivery of the documents, though he can get nothing out of them, and though in any intelligible sense no property in the goods can ever pass to him – i.e., if the goods have been lost by a peril excepted by the bill of lading, and by a peril not insured by the policy, the bill of lading and the policy yet being in the proper commercial form called for by the contract . . .' If the vendor fulfils his contract by shipping the appropriate goods in the appropriate manner under a proper contract of carriage, and if he also obtains the proper documents for tender to the purchaser, I am unable to see how the rights or duties of either party are affected by the loss of ship or goods, or by knowledge of such loss by the vendor, prior to actual tender of the documents.

Question

Generally in a c.i.f. contract, property in the goods passes on delivery of the bill of lading. Why cannot the buyer argue total failure of consideration where the goods have perished before the bill of lading is handed over?

4 Sellers' Duties as to Title

As we have seen, the fundamental obligation of the seller under the Sale of Goods Act is to transfer the *property* in the goods. If he fails to do this because a third party has a better title to the goods, then arguably there is a total failure of consideration and the 'sale' is no sale at all. The consequence is that even though the buyer may have had valuable use from the goods, he is still entitled to his money back. This conclusion was actually reached in *Rowland* v. *Divall*.[30] In the case of rapidly depreciating items, this confers an even greater benefit on the buyer.[31] In other words, although the title warranty is spelled out expressly in s. 12(1), it would seem to be superfluous to the extent that the very nature of a sale of goods under the Act requires the transfer of property. Furthermore, the consequence is that the normal compensatory principle of damages for breach of warranty contained in s. 53(2) does not seem to apply (indeed, the question of loss of the right of rejection does not appear to arise under s. 11(4)). The fallacy of *Rowland* v. *Divall* seems to stem from the word 'property'. Property does not mean 'ownership' in English law in the sense of 'dominium'. We are a relative title jurisdiction.[32] The seller in *Rowland* v. *Divall* did transfer something: a title good against all the world except the person with a better title. There was therefore a sale of goods. The goods had been physically delivered to the buyer, and he had accepted them. The matter should have proceeded as a question of damages for breach of warranty under s. 12(1) therefore, and the plaintiffs should have been limited to recovering his true loss, i.e. the usual principle of compensatory damages applied. This analysis avoids the problem of consumable goods: if the buyer has consumed the goods to which a third party had a better title, theoretically, on the *Rowland* v. *Divall* argument, he can *still* recover the price. The fact that s. 12(3) now makes it clear that there can be a contract under which a seller can transfer such title as he has seems to reinforce the argument that the concept of 'property' for the purposes of s. 2 of the Act as understood in *Rowland* v. *Divall* is wrong.[33]

Questions of title in the sense discussed above are not the only provenance of s. 12. At present, United Kingdom intellectual property

 DOI: 10.4324/9781003174615-5

rights[34] owned by third parties may result in the seller being liable for breach of s. 12. The following case illustrates this.

NIBLETT v. CONFECTIONERS' MATERIALS [1921] 3 K.B. 387

The sellers sold condensed milk tins to the buyers bearing labels which infringed the Nestlé trade mark. As a result the buyers had to remove the labels. They sued the seller for breach of s. 12(1).

ATKIN L.J.
In a contract for the sale of goods there is an implied condition that the seller has a right to sell the goods 'unless the circumstances of the contract are such as to show a different intention.' I think those words were inserted in s. 12 of the Sale of Goods Act to exclude sales by a sheriff under an execution and other cases where by implication or by express terms there is no warranty of title. In the present case I see no circumstances 'such as to show a different intention,' and therefore I think there was an implied condition that the sellers had a right to sell the goods. The sellers had not the right to sell these goods. They gave an undertaking not to sell them, and having admitted that they were an infringement of the Nestlé Company's trade mark they were liable to an injunction restraining the sale. Therefore they had no right to sell these goods at the time when the property was to pass. It may be that the implied condition is not broken if the seller is able to pass to the purchaser a right to sell notwithstanding his own inability; but that is not so here, for the Nestlé Company had the rights against the appellants as they had against the respondents. In my opinion there was a breach of this condition. The only doubt in my mind is raised by the judgement of Lord Russell C.J. in *Monforts* v. *Marsden* 12 R.P.C. 266. That was not a decision expressly under s. 12 of the Sale of Goods Act, 1893, because the sale took place before that Act was passed; but the Lord Chief Justice treated the Act as declaring the law at the date of the sale. He said: 'I think that all that the first implied condition as to title meant was that the man had a right to sell the thing as it was in the sense of being able to pass the property in the thing to the vendee, and in the sense that nobody had a title superior to that of the vendor, so that the possession of the vendee could be disturbed, unless title means no more than ability to pass the property, in which case it does not exhaust all the contingencies whereby the possession of the vendee can be disturbed. The owners of the patent had no right or ability to pass the property, but they had a right to disturb the possession of the defendant in that case. The Lord Chief Justice continued: 'In other words, it is a warranty of good title to the thing; it is not a covenant as to the quality of the thing, as to the workability of the thing, or that the machine shall be delivered under circumstances in which the vendee should be entitled to work it.' With all respect, this is to apply to a code a wrong canon of construction. The true canon is to give full effect to the words enacted, not to read those words by the light of existing decisions and infer from the absence of authority an intention not to

amend the law. Whatever the law may have been before the passing of the Sale of Goods Act, there is since that Act an implied condition that the sellers shall have a right to sell the goods at the time when the property is to pass. As they had not that right there was a breach of this condition.

I think there was also a breach of the implied warranty in sub-s. 2, that the buyer shall have and enjoy quiet possession of the goods. It may be that possession would not be disturbed if the only cause of complaint was that the buyer could not dispose of the goods, and that the warranty is confined to disturbance of possession of the goods delivered under the contract of sale. The warranty so interpreted was broken. The appellants were never allowed to have quiet possession. They had to strip off the labels before they could assume possession of the goods. Probably this warranty resembles the covenant for quiet enjoyment of real property by a vendor who conveys as beneficial owner in being subject to certain limitations, and only purports to protect the purchaser against lawful acts of third persons and against breaches of the contract of sale and tortious acts of the vendor himself. But it is unnecessary to define its scope. There was a clear breach in the present case.

Note

In this case the intellectual property rights existed at the time of the sale. If they arise later and as a result the buyer is disturbed in his quiet enjoyment of the goods, a breach of s. 12(2) may occur (see *Microbeads A.C.* v. *Vinhurst Road Markings Ltd*).[35]

5 Suppliers' Duties as to Description and Quality

Note

In this section sales by sample (s. 15) are not separately treated. The question of 'unmerchantable' under s. 15(2)(c) is the same as under 2. 14(2).

INTRODUCTION

The remedies in private law against suppliers of defective or deficient goods come from three sources: the law of contract (under which, of course, are subsumed the remedies provided by the Sale of Goods Act[36]), the law of tort (in particular the tort of negligence as it has developed since *Donoghue* v. *Stevenson*[37]) and, sitting somewhat awkwardly between the two, the remedies provided by the Misrepresentation Act, 1967.

The division between contract and tort is problematic. Historically, the remedy for the buyer of substandard goods was via the tort of deceit, which required either that the seller had knowingly made a false representation, or that he had 'warranted' the assertion.[38] From *Stuart* v. *Wilkins*,[39] originally for purely procedural reasons, plaintiffs began to plead their cases in *assumpsit* (i.e. contract). This did not at first make any substantive difference. However, following on from developments of the eighteenth century in relation to the title warranties,[40] the requirement that there be an express warranty rapidly disappeared. The courts began to imply a warranty that the goods should be of merchantable quality,[41] and that they should be fit for the purpose for which they were sold.[42] These warranties found their way into the Sale of Goods Act 1893. The relevant provisions imposing quality duties on a seller are contained in ss. 13-15. There they are called 'conditions'. The problem with that designation will be discussed in relation to remedies. For our present purposes the important thing to realise is that the Act firmly placed the warranties within the field of contract. Tort law developed along its own lines. The old tort of

DOI: 10.4324/9781003174615-6

deceit removed itself completely from the developments which had taken place within *assumpsit* and emerged as the modern tort of deceit or fraud.[43] Negligence law, after running parallel to *assumpsit* so far as the privity requirement was concerned in relation to the liability for defective products,[44] assumed its modern form after the leading case of *Donoghue* v. *Stevenson*.[45]

These developments have produced a number of anomalies. A manufacturer whose products are sold through ordinary retail outlets is liable only in negligence, or improbably deceit or fraud, for there is no privity of contract between him and the ultimate buyer.[46] The shop, on the other hand, is liable irrespective of negligence on the warranties imposed by the Act, though only to its actual customer, not to that customer's spouse or other third party whose only remedy for injury is in negligence.

The fact that the shop can start the process of suing back up the chain of sales which leads to the manufacturer, so that liability ultimately comes to rest on the responsible party, is no doubt one reason for holding that the liability under the quality warranties is absolute.[47] Unfortunately, whilst there are good reasons for holding a shop absolutely liable for defects they could not themselves possibly ascertain (and remember that in contract law the undertaking of an absolute liability presents no difficulties – you can promise that it will rain if you wish[48]), ultimately, in relation to the manufacturer, we may wish to hold that the liability is simply to provide a product as good as care and skill can make it in the present state of science.[49] Furthermore, even when a product is defective, we may not wish to hold the manufacturer liable. Do we, for example, hold the little manufacturer of an aircraft's altimeter liable for the loss of the whole plane, or do we leave the loss with the assembler of the aircraft?[50] It is on questions such as this that we reach the frontiers of traditional jurisprudence. In the United States, where the doctrine of privity has broken down, both because of the development of warranty liability in tort in a way which did not occur here, and the extension of liability under the Uniform Commercial Code,[51] these frontiers have been reached. In this country, because of the mould in which the law has set, we are quite a long way away, at present.

(1) THE SELLER'S DUTIES UNDER THE SALE OF GOODS ACT WARRANTIES

The warranties implied by the Sale of Goods Act, ss. 13-15 (correspondence with description, merchantability, fitness for purpose, correspondence with sample) raise a number of difficulties. Leaving aside sales by sample, the first problem with the warranties is defining the scope of each of them. The reason for this is partly historical. The original merchantable quality warranty[52] applied only where goods were bought by description from a seller who dealt in goods of that description. This had two consequences. The meaning of sale by description tended to be widened beyond the natural meaning of the words; so, for example, sales of specific articles displayed in shops would tend to be treated as falling within the term on the ground that the sale was in reality the sale of an article belonging to a class[53] (a not unreasonable approach, but not quite what was contemplated by the draftsman of the Act[54]). Furthermore, many cases which might more reasonably have been dealt with under the merchantable quality warranty were dealt with under the fitness for purpose warranty.[55] The original fitness for purpose warranty, moreover, was not implied in the contract for the sale of a specified article under its patent or trade name.[56] This led in some cases to a breach of the merchantable quality warranty being found, but not fitness for purpose, particularly as the request for the article under such designation might anyway negative the requirement of reliance on the seller's skill and judgement.[57] Whilst the Supply of Goods (Implied Terms) Act 1973 altered both sections to remove these requirements, the leading cases are on the old sections, and the previous wording (not to mention numbering)[58] must be borne in mind when reading them (s. 14(3) of the 1973 Act was amended by the Consumer Credit Act 1974 and the 1979 Act consolidates the amendment).

However, the problem of the division of labour between the sections is not the greatest difficulty. A central problem in approaching the application of the sections underlies all contract law, it is the extent to which we have regard to the subjective expectations and intentions of the parties. For example, A sells to B goods which he knows to be defective at an inflated price. B thinks that the goods are first-class and that he is getting a bargain. At common law the classic retort to B, if he complained, was 'caveat emptor'.[59] Once the courts had started to imply quality warranties, however, the problem immediately arose as to what precisely the obligations under those warranties were. There was a potential tension between, on the one hand, the principle which held that the parties themselves were the best judges, and if buyers wanted goods to possess particular qualities, they should stipulate for them (and buyers should not receive all our sympathy; they sometimes express disappointment at the quality of goods when their real complaint is that they do not want them any more); and on the other hand, the duties reasonably to be imposed on the seller in the absense of such stipulation.[60] One solution was for the courts to take an objective standpoint. What contract would the parties as reasonable men have made? To an extent this approach is the only possible one, and is embodied in s. 14(6):

> Goods of any kind are of merchantable quality within the meaning of subsection (2) if they are as fit for the purpose or purposes for which goods of that kind are bought as it is reasonable to expect having regard to any description applied to them, the price (if relevant) and all the other relevant circumstances.

When the buyer singles himself out from the generality of buyers by *making known* the particular purpose for which he is buying the goods, the subjective element comes into play. So far, so good, but beyond this point there is a dividing of the ways. The extreme objectivist will tend to disregard subjective indications of what the probable intentions and expectations of the parties were. He will ask what is the *ordinary* meaning of what was said? And what qualities *ordinarily* would be expected of such goods?[61] As Holmes observed in connection with the construction of contracts: 'I do not suppose that you could prove . . . that the words in a dispositive instrument making sense as they stand should have a different meaning from the common one; for instance, that the parties to a contract orally agreed that when they wrote five hundred feet it should mean one hundred inches, or that Bunker Hill Monument should signify the Old South Church.'[62] So in the context of sale of goods, the objectivist will want to disregard subjective considerations even if they suggest that goods which were objectively not of merchantable quality were subjectively fit for this particular buyer's purposes.[63] This approach underlies some of the sale by description cases such as *Arcos Ltd* v. *Ronaasen and Son*[64] and *re Moore and Landauer*.[65] If the contract said goods should correspond with a particular description, it is not open to the seller to supply goods which differ from that description even in quite minor respects. The buyer may reject. He does not have to show why the goods would not have suited his particular purposes, even though the reasonable inference is that they would have. The modern trend is something of a compromise. Lord Diplock in *Ashington Piggeries* v. *Christopher Hill*[66] asked 'What, if any, responsibility as to the characteristics of the goods to be supplied under the contract would the seller reasonably understand that the buyer believed that he, the seller, was accepting?', an approach which echoes the views expressed by the moral philosopher Paley.[67]

(a) Correspondence with description

(i) *What constitutes the description of goods?*

OSCAR CHESS v. WILLIAMS [1957] 1 W.L.R. 370

The defendant owned a Morris car which the registration book stated to be a 1948 model. He traded it in to the plaintiffs, who were motor dealers, in part-exchange for another vehicle. The plaintiffs' salesman was familiar with the car, and thought that it was a 1948 model. It was a 1939 model. The dealers sued for the difference in value. Denning L.J. stated the facts set out above, and said that in describing the car as a 1948 Morris the defendant was perfectly innocent; he honestly believed it was a 1948 model; and so no doubt did the previous sellers. Someone in 1948 must have fraudulently altered the log-book, but he could not now be traced.

His Lordship continued:

I entirely agree with the judge that both parties assumed that the Morris was a 1948 model and that this assumption was fundamental to the contract. But this does not prove that the representation was a term of the contract. The assumption was based by both of them on the date given in the registration book as the date of first registration. They both believed it was a 1948 model whereas it was only a 1939 one. They were both mistaken and their mistake was of fundamental importance.

The effect of such a mistake is this: it does not make the contract a nullity from the beginning, but it does in some circumstances enable the contract to be set aside in equity. If the buyer had come promptly, he might have succeeded in getting the whole transaction set aside in equity on the ground of this mistake: see *Solle* v. *Butcher* [1950] 1 K.B. 671; 66 T.L.R. (Pt. 1) 448; [1949] 2 All E.R. 1107; but he did not do so and it is now too late for him to do it; see *Leaf* v. *International Galleries* [1950] 2 K.B. 86; 66 T.L.R. (Pt. 1) 1031; [1950] 1 All E.R. 693. His only remedy is in damages, and to recover these he must prove a warranty.

In saying that he must prove a warranty, I use the word 'warranty' in its ordinary English meaning to denote a binding promise. Everyone knows what a man means when he says 'I guarantee it' or 'I warrant it' or 'I give you my word on it'. He means that he binds himself to it.

That is the meaning it has borne in English law for 300 years from the leading case of *Chandelor* v. *Lopus* (1603) Cro. Jac. 4 onwards. During the last 50 years, however, some lawyers have come to use the word 'warranty' in another sense. They use it to denote a subsidiary term in a contract as distinct from a vital term which they call a 'condition'. In so doing they depart from the ordinary meaning, not only of the word 'warranty' but also of the word 'condition'. There is no harm in their doing this, so long as they confine this technical use to its proper sphere, namely to distinguish between a vital term, the breach of which gives the right to treat the contract as at an end, and a subsidiary term which does not. But the trouble comes when one person uses the word 'warranty' in its ordinary meaning and another uses it in its technical meaning. When Holt C.J., in *Crosse* v. *Gardner* (1689) Carth. 90, as glossed by Buller J. in *Pasley* v. *Freeman* (1789) 3 Term Rep. 51, 57. and *Medina* v. *Stoughton*, (1699) 1 Salk. 210 made his famous ruling that an affirmation at the time of a sale is a warranty, provided it appears on evidence to be so intended, he used the word 'warranty' in its ordinary English meaning of a binding promise: and when Lord Haldane L.C. and Lord Moulton in 1913 in *Heilbut, Symons & Co.* v. *Buckleton*, [1913] A.C. 30, 38, 50, 51 adopted his ruling they used it likewise in its ordinary meaning. These different uses of the word seem to have been the source of confusion in the present case. The judge did not ask himself, 'Was the representation (that it was a 1948 Morris) intended to be a warranty?' He asked himself, 'Was it fundamental to the contract?' He answered it by saying that it was fundamental; and therefore it was a condition and not a warranty. By concentrating on whether it was fundamental, he seems to me to have missed the crucial point in the case which is whether it was a term of the contract at all. The crucial question is: was it a binding promise or only an innocent misrepresentation? The technical distinction between a 'condition' and a 'warranty' is quite immaterial in this case, because it is far too late for the buyer to reject the car. He can at best only claim damages. The material distinction here is between a statement which is a term of the contract and a statement which is only an innocent misrepresentation. This distinction is best expressed by the ruling of Lord Holt: Was it intended as a warranty or not? using the word warranty there in its ordinary English meaning: because it gives the exact shade of meaning that is required. It is something to which a man must be taken to bind himself.

In applying Lord Holt's test, however, some misunderstanding has arisen by the use of the word 'intended'. It is sometimes supposed that the tribunal must look into the minds of the parties to see what they themselves intended. That is a mistake. Lord Moulton made it quite clear that [1913] A.C. 30, 38, 50, 51 'The intention of the parties can only be deduced from the totality of the evidence'. The question whether a warranty was intended depends on the conduct of the parties, on their words and behaviour, rather than on their thoughts. If an intelligent bystander would reasonably infer that a warranty was intended, that will suffice. And this, when the facts are not in dispute, is a question of law. That is shown by *Heilbut, Symons & Co.* v. *Buckleton* [1913] A.C. 30 itself, where the House of Lords upset the finding by a jury of a warranty.

It is instructive to take some recent instances to show how the courts have approached this question. When the seller states a fact which is or should be within his own knowledge and of which the buyer is ignorant, intending that the buyer should act on it, and he does so, it is easy to infer a warranty: see *Couchman* v. *Hill* [1947] K.B. 554, 63 T.L.R. 81, where the former stated that the heifer was unserved, and *Harling* v. *Eddy* [1951] 2 K.B. 739; [1951] 2 T.L.R. 245; [1951] 2 All E.R. 212, where he stated that there was nothing wrong with her. So also if he makes a promise about something which is or should be within his own control: see *Birch* v. *Paramount Estates Ltd* Unreported: Oct. 2, 1956 (C.A.), decided on October 2, 1956, in this court, where the seller stated that the house would be as good as the show house. But if the seller, when he states a fact, makes it clear that he has no knowledge of his own but has got his information elsewhere, and is merely passing it on, it is not so easy to imply warranty. Such a case was *Routledge* v. *McKay* [1954] 1 W.L.R. 615, 636; [1954] 1 All E.R. 855 where the seller 'stated that it was a 1942 model and pointed to the corroboration found in the book,' and it was held that there was no warranty.

Turning now to the present case, much depends on the precise words that were used. If the seller says 'I believe it is a 1948 Morris. Here is the registration book to prove it' there is clearly no warranty. It is a statement of belief, not a contractual promise. But if the seller says 'I guarantee that it is a 1948 Morris. This is borne out by the registration book, but you need not rely on that. I give you my own guarantee that it is', there is clearly a warranty. The seller is making himself contractually responsible, even though the registration book is wrong.

In this case much reliance was placed by the judge on the fact that the buyer looked up Glass's Guide and paid £290 on the footing that it was a 1948 model: but that fact seems to me to be neutral. Both sides believed the car to have been made in 1948 and in the belief the buyer paid £290. That belief can be just as firmly based on the buyer's own inspection of the log-book as on a contractual warranty by the seller.

Once that fact is put on one side I ask myself: What is the proper inference from the known facts? It must have been obvious to both that the seller had himself no personal knowledge of the year when the car was made. He only became owner after a great number of changes. He must have been relying on the registration book. It is unlikely that such a person would warrant the year of manufacture. The most he would do would be to state his belief, and then produce the registration book in verification of it. In these circumstances the intelligent bystander would, I suggest, say that the seller did not intend to bind himself so as to warrant that it was a 1948 model. If the seller was asked to pledge himself to it, he would at once have said 'I cannot do that. I have only the log-book to go by, the same as you.'

The judge seems to have thought that there was a difference between written contracts and oral contracts. He thought that the reason why the buyer failed in *Heilbut, Symons & Co.* v. *Buckleton* [1913] A.C. 30 and *Routledge* v. *McKay* [1954] 1 W.L.R. 615 was because the sales were afterwards recorded in writing, and the written contract contained no reference to the representation. I agree that there was an important factor in those cases. If an oral representation is afterwards recorded in writing, it is good evidence that it was intended as a warranty. If it is not put into writing, it is evidence against a warranty being intended. But it is by no means decisive. There have been many cases where the courts have found an oral warranty collateral to a written contract such as *Birch* v. *Paramount Estates* Unreported: Oct. 2, 1956 (C.A.). But when the purchase is not recorded in writing at all it must not be supposed that every representation made in the course of the dealing is to be treated as a warranty. The question then is still: Was it intended as a warranty? In the leading case of *Chandelor* v. *Lopus* Cro. Jac 4. in 1603 a man by word of mouth sold a precious stone for £100 affirming it to be a bezoar stone whereas it was not. The declaration averred that the seller affirmed it to be a bezoar stone, but did not aver that he warranted it to be so. The declaration was held to be ill because 'the bare affirmation that it was a bezoar stone, without warranting it to be so, is no cause of action'. That has been the law from that day to this and it was emphatically reaffirmed by the House of Lords in *Heilbut, Symons & Co.* v. *Buckleton* [1913] A.C. 30, 38, 50.

One final word: It seems to me clear that the motor-dealers who bought the car relied on the year stated in the log-book. If they had wished to make sure of it, they could have checked it then and there, by taking the engine number and chassis number and writing to the makers. They did not do so at the time, but only eight months later. They are experts, and, not having made that check at the time, I do not think they should now be allowed to recover against the innocent seller who produced to them all the evidence he had, namely, the registration book. I agree that it is hard on the dealers to have paid more than the car is worth: but it would be equally hard on the seller to make him pay the difference. He would never have bought the Hillman at all unless he had got the allowance of £290 for the Morris. The best course in all these cases would be to 'shunt' the difference down the train of innocent sellers until one reaches the rogue who perpetrated the fraud: but he can rarely be traced, or if he can, he rarely has the money to pay the damages. So one is left to decide between a number of innocent people who is to bear the loss. That can only be done by applying the law about representations and warranties as we know it: and that is what I have tried to do. If the rogue can be traced, he can be sued by whomsoever has suffered the loss; but if he cannot be traced, the loss must lie where it falls. It should not be inflicted on innocent sellers, who sold the car many months, perhaps many years before, and have forgotten all about it and have conducted their affairs on the basis that the transaction was concluded. Such a seller would not be able to recollect after all this length of time the exact words he used, such as whether he said 'I believe it is a 1948 model' or 'I warrant it is a 1948 model'. The right course is to let the buyer set aside the transaction if he finds out the mistake quickly and comes promptly before other interests have irretrievably intervened; otherwise the loss must lie where it falls: and that is, I think, the course prescribed by law. I would allow this appeal accordingly.

Note

Arguably this case involved a barter and not a sale (see Chapter 1); certainly s. 13, Sale of Goods Act is not discussed. The case has been included, however, because Lord Denning's discussion of warranties is valuable. The principle of the case fits well with Lord Diplock's approach to the merchantable quality warranty. The 'seller' was a layman, and laymen do not expect experts to rely on them for matters within their own field of expertise.

(ii) *What is correspondence with description?*

Quantities

ARCOS v. RONAASEN [1933] A.C. 470

The contract specified ¼-inch and the rest 1/2-9/16-inch or 1/2-5/8-inch. It was found as fact that the goods were of merchantable quality within the contract description and fit for making cement barrels.

LORD ATKIN

It was contended that in all commercial contracts the question was whether there was a 'substantial' compliance with the contract: there always must be some margin: and it is for the tribunal of fact to determine whether the margin is exceeded or not. I cannot agree. If the written contract specifies conditions of weight, measurement and the like, those conditions must be complied with. A ton does not mean about a ton, or a yard about a yard. Still less when you descend to minute measurements does ½-inch mean about ½-inch. If the seller wants a margin he must and in my experience does stipulate for it. Of course by recognized trade usage particular figures may be given a different meaning, as in a baker's dozen; or there may be even incorporated a definite margin more or less: but there is no evidence or finding of such a usage in the present case.

RE MOORE & CO. LTD and LANDAUER & CO. [1921] A.C. 519

The contract specified canned fruit packed in cases containing thirty tins each. The seller delivered the right quantity of tins but some were packed in cases of twenty-four tins. There was no difference between the market value of the goods when packed in twenty-four-tin cases. The buyer rejected. *Held*: he was entitled to do so under s. 30(3).

SCRUTTON L.J.
In the present case for some reason the sellers and buyers have put into their contract: 'About 3100 cases with 30 tins to the case.' They have put that in as a description, and that is what the sellers must tender to the buyers. The umpire finds that twenty-four tins to the case are as valuable commercially as thirty tins to the case. That may be so. Yet a man who has bought under a contract thirty tins to the case may have sold under the same description, and may be placed in considerable difficulty by having goods tendered to him which do not comply with the description under which he bought, or under which he has resold.

Questions

1. Can you reconcile these cases with the approach adopted in *Cehave* v. *Bremer Handelsgesellschaft* (p. 116, below)?
2. Is not Scrutton L.J.'s argument about a possible sub-sale tautologous?

Qualities other than quantities or other measurements

ASHINGTON PIGGERIES v. CHRISTOPHER HILL LTD [1972] A.C. 441

The facts are set out at p. 71 below.

LORD DILHORNE
The line between a difference in quality and a difference in kind may in many instances be difficult to draw. Here, where the distinction is between poisonous and non-poisonous herring meal, that was, in my opinion, more than a difference in quality, and I agree with Milmo J. in thinking that there was difference in kind and so a breach of section 13.

The same question arises for decision in relation to the respondents' claim under section 13 as arose on the appellants' claim against the respondents. For the reasons I have already stated, and which I need not repeat, in my opinion the difference between Norwegian herring meal, which is normally harmless to animals, and Norwegian herring meal and containing DMNA in sufficient quantities as to be harmful to animals is not just a difference of quality but one of kind and I would, therefore, find in favour of the respondents on this issue.

The other Lords disagreed:

LORD WILBERFORCE
Whether in a given case a substance in or upon which there has been produced by chemical interaction some additional substance can properly be described or, if one prefers the word, identified, as the original substance qualified by the addition of a past participle such as

contaminated or oxidised, or as the original substance plus, or intermixed with, an additional substance, may, if pressed to analysis, be a question of an Aristotelian character. Where does a substance with a quality pass into an aggregate of substances? I do not think that it can be solved by asking whether the chemical interaction came about by some natural or normal process, e.g., preservation by the addition of salt (sodium chloride), or by some alien intrusion by the production of DMNA from sodium nitrite through a heating effect. I cannot see any distinction in principle in this difference. Further I do not believe that the Sale of Goods Act was designed to provoke metaphysical discussions as to the nature of what is delivered in comparison with what is sold. The test of description, at least where commodities are concerned, is intended to be a broader, more commonsense, test of a mercantile character. The question whether that is what the buyer bargained for has to be answered according to such tests as men in the market would apply, leaving more delicate questions of condition, or quality, to be determined under other clauses of the contract or sections of the Act. Perhaps this is to admit an element of impression into the decision, but I think it is more than impression which leads me to prefer the answer, if not all of the reasoning of the Court of Appeal that the defect in the meal was a matter of quality or condition rather than of description. I think that buyers and sellers and arbitrators in the market, asked what this was, could only have said that the relevant ingredient was herring meal and, therefore, that there was no failure to correspond with description. In my opinion, the appellants do not succeed under section 13.

Note

The impregnated dates in *Asfar* v. *Blundell* (p. 25, above) could arguably therefore still properly have been described as 'dates', their fitness for human consumption, or no doubt enhanced fitness for conversion into fertiliser, being a question of quality.

(b) Merchantable quality and fitness for purpose

These sections are taken together. For the reasons given in the introduction to this section (p. 53) it is difficult to separate the cases in a coherent way.

(i) *The problem of products liability generally*

In the United States, as was pointed out in the introduction to this section, strict tort liability has developed parallel to the warranty liability in contract. The problems, however, of deciding whether or not the producer is to be held liable are ultimately the same.

ON THE NATURE OF STRICT TORT LIABILITY FOR PRODUCTS by John W. Wade (1973) 44 Miss. L.J. 825, 837

If there is agreement that the determination of whether a product is unreasonably dangerous, or is not duly safe, involves the necessary application of a standard, it will, like the determination of negligence or of strict liability for an abnormally dangerous activity, require the consideration and weighing of a number of factors. I offer here a revised list of factors which seem to me to be of significance in applying the standard:

(1) The usefulness and desirability of the product – its utility to the user and to the public as a whole.

(2) The safety aspects of the product – the likelihood that it will cause injury, and the probable seriousness of the injury.

(3) The availability of a substitute product which would meet the same need and not be as unsafe.

(4) The manufacturer's ability to eliminate the unsafe character of the product without impairing its usefulness or making it too expensive to maintain its utility.

(5) The user's ability to avoid danger by the exercise of care in the use of the product.

(6) The user's anticipated awareness of the dangers inherent in the product and their avoidability, because of general public knowledge of the obvious condition of the product, or of the existence of suitable warnings or instructions.

(7) The feasibility, on the part of the manufacturer, of spreading the loss by setting the price of the product or carrying liability insurance.

Note

In *U.S.* v. *Carroll Towing Co* 159 F. 2d 169, Learned Hand C.J. suggested that the duty of care in negligence is a function of three variables: (1) the probability of harm; (2) the gravity of the resulting injury; (3) the burden of adequate precautions. On this view a manufacturer's strict tort liability as analysed above, and negligence liability, may depend upon similar considerations.

Bear these factors in mind when studying the cases in the following section. To what extent do the judges seem intuitively to be taking such factors into account?

(ii) *Products liability under the Sale of Goods Act*

S. 14(2) applies to goods 'supplied' under the contract, i.e. not merely to the goods actually forming the subject-matter of the sale.

WILSON v. RICKETT COCKERILL [1954] 1 Q.B. 598

The defendants sold to the plaintiffs a quantity of Coalite. A fire made up with some of the Coalite exploded due to a piece of coal with explosive embedded into it which had been delivered with the Coalite.

DENNING L.J.
The judge for himself would have held that the plaintiffs could have recovered, but he felt that he ought to follow a decision of the Court of Session in Scotland, *Duke* v. *Jackson* 1921 S.C. 362. In that case a bag of household coal purchased from a coal merchant contained a detonator which exploded while the coal was being burned in the kitchen fire. The householder lost his eye, but the Court of Session held that, on the facts alleged in the pleadings, there was no breach of the condition implied under section 14(1) of the Sale of Goods Act, 1893. The reasoning of the Court of Session was after this wise: the coal, as coal, was all right; it was fit for its purpose; the trouble was that there was something in it which the householder did not purchase, namely, a detonator; and as he did not purchase it, he could not complain of it as a breach of contract under section 14(1); but only for negligence, if there was any.

With all respect to the Court of Session, I must confess that I do not understand this line of reasoning. Coal is not bought by the lump. It is bought by the sack or by the hundredweight or by the ton. The consignment is delivered as a whole and must be considered as a whole; not in bits. A sack of coal, which contains hidden in it a detonator, is not fit for burning, and no sophistry should lead us to believe that it is fit.

The Court of Session were referred to the English case of the milk which contained typhoid germs, *Frost* v. *Aylesbury Dairy Co. Ltd*, [1905] 1 K.B. 608; 21 T.L.R. where this court held that the buyer was entitled to recover damages; but the Scottish court pushed that case on one side on the ground that all the milk there was contaminated, whereas none of the coal was unfit; only the detonator. Again, I am afraid I cannot follow the reasoning. I can see no distinction in principle between liquids and solids. If the admixture of an injurious ingredient makes a liquid unfit for drinking, so does the admixture of an injurious detonator make coal unfit for burning. It is no answer for the seller to say that there was nothing wrong with the coal, as coal. There was a great deal wrong with the consignment as a consignment.

It is to be noticed that the Court of Session were not referred to another case in this court, *Chaproniere* v. *Mason*, (1905) 21 T.L.R. 633 where a bath bun had a stone in it and the solicitor, who bought it, broke his tooth upon it. Lord Collins M.R. said that, speaking for himself, he would be inclined to say that such a bun was not reasonably fit for mastication. He was perhaps unduly hesitant when he said he was 'inclined to say.'

In these circumstances, I think that we should not adopt the reasoning of the Court of Session, but should see how the matter stands on the sections of the Act. The principal point made before us was that section 14 does not apply to this case, because both subsections (1) and (2), it was said, only refer to the contract goods, that is, to the goods which are the subject of the contract of sale: and, so here, it refers only to the Coalite proper and not to the explosive piece which was in it.

The answer to that argument lies in the opening words of section 14, which show that the section refers to the 'goods supplied under a contract of sale.' In my opinion that means the goods delivered in purported pursuance of the contract. The section applies to all goods so delivered, whether they conform to the contract or not: that is, in this case, to the whole consignment, including the offending piece, and not merely to the Coalite alone.

The following three cases are the leading House of Lords authorities on the quality warranties:

KENDALL v. LILLICO [1969] 2 A.C. 31

Kendall sold Brazilian groundnut extract to Grimsdale. Grimsdale sold to SAPPA who compounded animal feedstuffs. SAPPA used the extract to make feed for young pheasants. Hardwick Game Farm bought some of this feed. Much Brazilian groundnut extract contained a poison, aflatoxin. Many of Hardwick Game Farm's young birds died, and the cause of death was subsequently traced to this poison. At the time when SAPPA manufactured the feed, it was not known that Brazilian groundnut extract contained this poison. By the date of the trial, the danger was well known, and the extract readily marketable since it was suitable for cattle feed, though not for poultry feed.

Held: (1) Grimsdale had broken the implied condition of fitness for purpose in their sale to SAPPA;

(2) That Kendall had also broken this implied term and (Lord Guest dissenting) that common membership of a trade association was not sufficient to rebut the presumption that Grimsdale had relied on Kendall's skill and judgment;

(3) (Lord Pearce dissenting and Lord Wilberforce expressing no opinion) that none of the sellers had broken the implied condition of merchantable quality.

LORD REID

Kendall and Grimsdale are both members of the London Cattle Food Traders' Association. Brazilian groundnuts had not been imported until 1959 but early in 1960 there were large shipments. Kendall had acquired a large quantity and while the goods were afloat Kendall sold a considerable quantity in the London Market to Grimsdale. Then Grimsdale sold a part of this to SAPPA at the market at Bury St Edmunds; SAPPA took delivery shortly after the arrival of the goods in London.

The case raises a number of points and I shall first consider the position under the Sale of Goods Act, 1893, section 14. The relevant subsections are:

'(1) Where the buyer, expressly or by implication, makes known to

> the seller the particular purpose for which the goods are required, so as to show that the buyer relies upon the seller's skill or judgment and the goods are of a description which it is in the course of the seller's business to supply (whether he be the manufacturer or not), there is an implied condition that the goods shall be reasonably fit for such purpose, provided that in the case of a contract for the sale of a specified article under its patent or other trade name, there is implied condition as to its fitness for any particular purpose. (2) Where goods are bought by description from a seller who deals in goods of that description (whether he be the manufacturer or not), there is an implied condition that the goods shall be of merchantable quality; provided that if the buyer has examined the goods, there shall be no implied condition as regards defects which such examination ought to have revealed': . . .

Conflicting arguments have been submitted about the meaning of almost every part of these subsections. If one puts aside for the moment the encrustations of authority their meaning appears to me to be reasonably clear. But, if a whole chapter of the law is compressed into one section of a code, one cannot expect its words to apply to unusual cases without expansion or adaptation. That is the task of the court: but it is not in my view legitimate to substitute for the words of the code some general words used by an eminent judge in a particular case and treat them as a test of universal application. Where that has been done in other chapters of the law it has led to trouble, and there has been a tendency to do that here.

I take first subsection (2) because it is of more general application. It applies to all sales by description where the seller deals in such goods. There may be a question whether the sale of a particular article is not really a sale by description but that does not arise here: these are clearly sales by description. Then it is a condition (unless excluded by the contract) that the goods must be of merchantable quality. Merchantable can only mean commercially saleable. If the description is a familiar one it may be that in practice only one quality of goods answers that description – then that quality and only that quality is merchantable quality. Or it may be that various qualities of goods are commonly sold under that description – then it is not disputed that the lowest quality commonly so sold is what is meant by merchantable quality: it is commercially saleable under that description. I need not consider here what expansion or adaptation of the statutory words is required where there is a sale of a particular article or a sale under a novel description. Here the description groundnut extractions had been in common use.

The novel feature of this case is that whereas in 1960 there appears to have been thought to be only one quality of this product, subject to minor variations, it has now been discovered that particular parcels though apparently of the usual quality may really be of a very different quality because they are contaminated by minute qualities of a powerful poison. So the question at once arises – do you judge merchantable quality in light of what was known at the time of the sale or in light of later knowledge?

It is quite clear that some later knowledge must be brought in for otherwise it would never be possible to hold that goods were unmerchantable by reason of latent defect. By definition a latent defect is something that could not have been discovered at the time by any examination which in light of then existing knowledge it was reasonable to make. But there is a question as to how much later knowledge ought to be brought in. In the present case it had become well known before the date of the trial that the defect was that these Brazilian groundnut extractions were contaminated by poison: but it had also become well known that, while this poison made the goods unsuitable for inclusion in food for poultry, it was generally regarded as proper to include such extractions in cattle food, provided that the proportion included did not exceed 5 per cent of the whole. The question is whether this latter fact should be taken into account in deciding whether these goods were of merchantable quality in 1960.

I think it would be very artificial to bring in some part of the later knowledge and exclude other parts. In this case it is quite true that there was a period, after the nature and effect of this contamination had been discovered but before it had become accepted that small quantities of contaminated goods could safely be included in cattle foods, during which contaminated groundnut extractions were virtually unsaleable. But suppose that in this case it had been discovered at an early stage that these goods could be used for cattle food, so that there never was a period during which they were unsaleable. In that case I would not think it possible to take into account the nature of the defect but to exclude from consideration the effect which knowledge of the defect had on the market.

There is clear evidence that before the date of the trial Indian groundnut extractions so contaminated were sold under the ordinary description and were not rejected by the buyers when the contamination was discovered; a director of British Oil and Cake Mills who are by far the largest compounders in this country said that they bought these goods untested and then tested them. If they were found to be very highly contaminated they were destroyed: but otherwise they were included in feeding stuffs for cattle. This company apparently did not claim any relief on the ground that such goods were of defective quality or were of no use if highly contaminated. And it appears that other buyers who found poison in the goods which they bought did not try to reject the goods but merely asked for rebates on the price: they never got any rebates and the evidence is that they did not press their claims. So I think that it sufficiently appears that groundnut extractions contaminated to an extent not said to be different from the contamination of the Brazilian product were regarded as of merchantable quality under the ordinary description at the date of the trial.

I do not think I am precluded from taking this view of the meaning of subsection (2) by any of the authorities. . .

On the face of it section 14(1) has a narrower scope. It requires that the buyers shall have required the goods for a particular purpose, and that purpose shall have been made known to the seller, and that it shall have been made known to him in such circumstances that he realised or ought to have realised that the buyer was relying on his using his skill or judgment to select goods fit for that purpose. Many cases in which the seller has been held liable under this subsection might equally well and more logically have been decided under subsection (2). But there has been a tendency to construe subsection (2) too narrowly and to compensate for that by giving a wide construction to subsection (1).

If the object of the disclosure of the particular purpose is, as I think it must be, to give to the seller an opportunity to exercise his skill or judgment in making or selecting appropriate goods, then it is difficult to see how a stated purpose can be a 'particular' purpose if it is stated so widely that it would cover different qualities of goods, because carrying out the purpose in one way would only require a lower quality of goods whereas carrying it out in another way would require a higher quality. Different qualities normally sell at different prices. If a customer sought from a manufactuer or dealer cloth for the purpose of making overcoats the dealer could not know what quality was required. A cut-price tailor would not want to pay the price of cloth used in Savile Row, and the tailor in Savile Row would not use the quality which the cut-price tailor wants. Unless the seller knew the nature of the buyer's business his only clue to the quality which the buyer wanted would be the price which the buyer was prepared to pay. If a high price was offered it might no doubt be right to hold that he must supply goods suitable for high quality coats. But it could not be right that if the cloth was sold at a price appropriate for the lower quality, the dealer would have to supply a higher quality simply because the buyer had stated that his purpose was to make overcoats and the lower quality would not always be reasonably fit for making every kind of overcoat.

It was argued that, whenever any purpose is stated so as to bring this subsection into operation, the seller must supply goods reasonably fit to enable the buyer to carry out his purpose in any normal way. But that can only be right if the purpose is stated with sufficient particularity to enable the seller to exercise his skill or judgment in making or selecting appropriate goods. The seller may know or be told that the merchant who is buying from him is buying for the purpose of reselling the goods in the course of his business. That may be sufficient to enable the seller to select appropriate goods or it may not. If the buyer's trade is such that some of his customers will want goods of the description which he is buying from the seller for one purpose or of one quality, and others of his customers will want goods of that description of another quality for another purpose, it could not be right that the buyer, merely by stating that he wants the goods for resale in the course of his business, could impose on the seller the obligation to supply goods reasonably fit for resale to every ordinary customer of the buyer no matter what his requirement might be.

Perhaps the solution of this problem is to be found in the application of the requirement of the section that the particular purpose must be made known 'so as to show that the buyer relied upon the seller's skill or judgment.' A buyer who is buying for the purpose – known to the seller – of reselling in the course of his business may want superior goods for which some of his customers will pay a high price, or he may want goods of lower quality to sell to less demanding customers. If he does not say which he wants, or at least indicate which he wants by the price he is offering, how can he be relying on the seller to supply something reasonably fit for his purpose? . . .

There is no doubt that in this case Kendall knew that Grimsdale were buying the goods to resell to compounders of animal feeding stuffs. In 1960 that was in my view a particular purpose because there is not evidence to show that it was not sufficiently particular to enable Kendall to exercise skill and judgment. It would not have helped Kendall to be told that the goods were ultimately to be fed to any particular kind or age of animal because at that time nobody knew that what was suitable for one kind of animal might not be suitable for another. Both Kendall and Grimsdale would assume that Grimsdale's customers would only include a suitable proportion in the particular food they were compounding; if they caused damage by using a wrong formula for their product neither Grimsdale nor Kendall would be responsible for that.

The difficult question is whether the circumstances were such as to show that Grimsdale were relying on Kendall's skill and judgment: but before I come to that there are two other matters which require some explanation. If the law were always logical one would suppose that a buyer, who has obtained a right to rely on the seller's skill and judgment, would only obtain thereby an assurance that proper skill and judgment had been exercised, and would only be entitled to a remedy if a defect in the goods was due to failure to exercise such skill and judgment. But the law has always gone farther than that. By getting the seller to undertake to use his skill and judgment the buyer gets under section 14(1) an assurance that the goods will be reasonably fit for his purpose and that covers not only defects which the seller ought to have detected but also defects which are latent in the sense that even the utmost skill and judgment on the part of the seller would not have detected them. It is for that reason that, if section 14(1) applies, Grimsdale are entitled to relief even though Kendall had no reason to suspect that the goods might be poisoned.

Secondly it is not necessary to decide whether today it would be a sufficiently particular purpose for Kendall to know that Grimsdale intended to resell to compounders of feeding stuffs. Today some compounders are willing to buy infected goods but presumably some are not, and I doubt whether mere knowledge on the part of Kendall that Grimsdale intended to resell would oblige Kendall to supply goods free from this poison. I would readily accept that a customer buying from an apparently reputable shop-keeper or from a manufacturer will normally as a matter of fact be relying on the seller's skill and judgment unless there is something to exclude the inference. But I do not think that the same can be said when two merchants equally knowledgeable deal with each other. Then I can see no reason in law or in fact for any presumption either way.

If one merchant merely acquired from an importer by buying on c.i.f. documents goods from a normal source and then resold to another merchant by transfer of the c.i.f. documents before taking delivery, there might then be little or no reason to suppose that the former merchant had exercised or could have exercised any skill or judgment with regard to the quality of the goods or that the latter was relying on him. But that was not the position in this case. Kendall had acquired these goods from a new source and one would suppose must have exercised skill and judgment in deciding to buy them and put them on the market. And the evidence appears to me to show that Kendall were recommending them to Grimsdale. In order to bring this subsection into operation it is not necessary to show that the parties consciously applied their minds to the question. It is enough that a reasonable seller in the shoes of Kendall would have realised that he was inviting Grimsdale to rely on his skill and judgment and that is what I think that in fact Kendall were doing. . . If that is right then section 14(1) did apply to this case.

Question

Do you think that there is an inconsistency in holding that these goods were merchantable in the light of later knowledge, but that nevertheless they were unfit for the purpose for which they were sold? See Lord Pearce, below.

Lord Guest dissented on the view that common membership of the London Cattle Food Trade Association was not sufficient to rebut the presumption that the third parties as buyers relied on the skill and judgment of the sellers for the purposes of the fitness for purpose warranty:

LORD GUEST

The particular purpose must be made known 'so as to show that the buyer relies on the seller's skill and judgment'. I have difficulty in acceding to what I understand to be the views of the rest of your Lordships on this point.

I can well understand where the sale is by a manufacturer or a retailer to a customer that the inference can easily be drawn. But Grimsdale and Kendall . . . were all dealers on the London Cattle Food Trade Market buying and selling goods of the same description possibly on the same day, certainly from day to day. The section may apply to dealers *inter se* as *Shields* v. *Honeywell & Stein Ltd* [1953] 1 Lloyd's Rep. 357, C.A., shows. But there is an air of unreality, in my view, in the idea that either of these dealers relied on the other's skill and judgment. It may well be that they trusted each other's honesty, as one of them said, but that is not the same thing as relying on each other's skill and judgment to select goods suitable for the particular purpose for which they were required. There is, in my view, great force in the judgment of Diplock L.J. in the Court of Appeal [1966] 1 W.L.R. 287, 332-336, when he analyses his reasons for saying that the implied warranty in section 14(1) did not apply to ordinary sales between dealers on the London Cattle Food Trade Market, and I respectfully agree with his conclusion.

Question

Do you think that Lord Guest's views are tenable on the present wording of the fitness for purpose warranty (s. 14(3))?

Lord Pearce dissented on the finding that the goods were of merchantable quality.

LORD PEARCE

Sir Owen Dixon was clearly right in saying [*Australian Knitting Mills* v. *Grant* 50 C.L.R. 387, 418] that in order to judge merchantability one must assume a knowledge of hidden defects, although these do not manifest themselves or are not discovered until some date later than the date of delivery which is the time as at which one must estimate merchantability. (See also Atkin L.J. in *Niblett Ltd* v. *Confectioners Materials Co. Ltd* [1921] 3 K.B. 387, 404: 'No one who knew the facts would buy them in that state or condition; in other words they were unsaleable and unmerchantable.') But what additional after-acquired knowledge must one assume? Logic might seem to indicate that the court should bring to the task all the after-acquired knowledge which it possesses at the date of trial. But I do not think that this is always so. For one is trying to find what market the goods would have had if their subsequently ascertained condition had been known. As it is a hypothetical exercise, one must create a hypothetical market. Never-the-less the hypothetical market should be one that could have existed, not one which could not have existed at the date of delivery. Suppose goods contained a hidden deadly poison to which there was discovered by scientists two years after delivery a simple, easy, inexpensive antidote which could render the goods harmless. They would be unmarketable at the date of delivery if the existence of the poison was brought to light, since no purchaser could then have known the antidote to the poison. Hypothesis is no reason for complete departure from possibility. One must keep the hypothesis in touch with the facts as far as possible. But I do not think that the point is important on the present facts.

In the present case, if on the day of delivery one had immediately compounded from it and fed the mixture from it to turkeys or young chickens or young pheasants it appears from the evidence that the birds would have died. One would then have had to label the goods for the market 'This food contains toxin so that if compounded in normal proportions it is fatal to turkeys, young chickens, or young pheasants or ducklings.' And also, I think, 'The nature of and strength of the toxin are unknown.' I find it hard to believe that there was on the date of delivery a market for it so labelled without abatement of price, even without the addition of the last sentence. On such evidence as there is it seems unlikely.

There is a further important point which the judge, I think, disregarded. The above argument is on the basis that the goods had a label setting out the courts' after-acquired knowledge of their toxin. But goods sold as fit for food and containing toxin of which no mention is made are quite different from goods which are labelled with a warning. Food which will be consumed by humans generally may be merchantable even though it will be dangerous to young children, provided, but only provided, that clear warning of that fact is given (or that the fact is so universally known that a warning is unnecessary). Food which was thought to be innocuous and whose normal purpose was for general consumption by cattle and poultry would be a hidden trap if unknown to the buyers it was lethal when used on some classes of its potential consumers. Thus the absence of a warning was in itself a serious defect, which can make goods unmerchantable even though they would have been merchantable if sold with due notice of the hidden defect. On this point it is irrelevant to consider whether, with a warning, it would have found buyers at the price. In my opinion, the real question for the court to consider is whether this groundnut meal with its particular toxicity but *without any warning to buyers* was merchantable as groundnut meal, which normally was fit for consumption by cattle and poultry without discrimination.

Question

To what extent do you think the outcome of this case might have been different had the definition of merchantable quality contained in s. 14(6) applied?

ASHINGTON PIGGERIES LTD v. CHRISTOPHER HILL LTD [1972] A.C. 441

The plaintiffs (respondents) supplied a formula for mink food devised by their Mr Udall to the defendants (appellants) who were compounders of animal foodstuffs. The feed made and supplied to the plaintiffs included Norwegian herring-meal bought from the third parties, which was contaminated with a chemical DMNA. It was not proved that the herring-meal was unfit for other animals, but it was unfit for mink. Many of the defendants' mink died.

The plaintiffs sued for the price of the feed supplied. The defendants counterclaimed for breach of ss. 13 and 14, Sale of Goods Act. The plaintiffs joined the Norwegian suppliers of the herring meal as third parties.

Held: (1) The plaintiffs were in breach of the fitness for purpose warranty;

(2) They were also in breach of the merchantable quality warranty (Lord Hodson and Lord Diplock dissented);

(3) That the third parties had broken the warranty of merchantability (Lord Diplock dissented).

(As to the liability under s. 13, see p. 60 above.)

LORD WILBERFORCE

The equation is, therefore, this: that DMNA is inherently and generally toxic: that as included in the relevant herring-meal it poisoned the appellants' mink: that this poisoning was not due to any specific idiosyncrasy among mink: that its effect on other species of subspecies is not accurately known beyond that it is potentially deleterious at least to the liver and that most normal species are more tolerant of it than mink.

In my opinion, the appellants made good their case: they proved the cause of their losses to lie in the inclusion of a generally (viz. non-specific as regards mink) toxic ingredient in the food. It was not for them to show that this same food killed, or poisoned, other species. So to require would place far too high a burden on a buyer. The buyer may have no means of ascertaining what the effect on other species may be. The whole of the contaminated consignment may have been fed to the buyer's animals: is the buyer to fail because he cannot show that this particular consignment killed, or at least injured, other animals? He must, I think, carry his proof to the point of showing that the guilty ingredient has some generally (as opposed to specifically) toxic quality. But once he has done this, has he not shown, at least with strong *prima facie* force, that a feeding stuff which contained it was unsuitable? Is he not entitled to throw on to the seller the burden of showing, if he can, that the damage to the buyer's animals was due to some factor within the field of responsibility reserved to the buyer? I would answer yes to these questions. In the end, it is for the judge to decide whether, on the evidence, the buyers have proved their case. Milmo J.'s conclusions are expressed in three passages, one in the main action, the others in the third party proceedings (the whole case was heard together):

> 'Herring meal does not normally contain a poison. The herring meal which killed the English mink contained DMNA which is a poison, and it contained it at a level sufficiently high to be lethal to mink, which are animals to which herring meal can properly be fed. All animals are sensitive to DMNA poisoning, though mink are more sensitive than most.' ([1968] 1 Lloyd's Rep. 457, 481.)
>
> 'I find that the meal which poisoned the English mink was not reasonably fit for use as an ingredient in animal foodstuffs because of the fact that it contained in substantial and significant quantities

DMNA which is a toxic substance to which all animals are sensitive.' (p. 487.)

'While I accept that there was no evidence that the meal *had a deleterious effect* upon any animal or other type of livestock other than mink, I do not consider that it was proved affirmatively that the meal which killed the mink *could have been fed with impunity* to all other types of livestock.' (p. 486 – emphasis supplied.)

This is precisely the position: coupled with the general finding as to toxicity (something to which all animals are sensitive, i.e., liable to suffer liver damage) it amounts to a rejection of the only line of defence open to the respondents – namely, that the relevant consignment was fit to be fed to all normal animals and only unfit to be fed to mink.

In my opinion, these findings were justified and correct.

So, all other elements being present as I have tried to show, I would hold that section 14(1) applies to the present case. I would agree with the judge that section 14(2) equally applies and disagree with the reasons (based on the 'description' argument) which led the Court of Appeal to a contrary opinion.

That the goods were unmerchantable was conceded in both courts – in my opinion, rightly so. Goods may quite well be unmerchantable even if 'purpose built'. Lord Wright made this quite clear in the *Cammell Laird* case [1934] A.C. 402; so equally with 'King Size' mink food.

He went on to deal with the alleged breach of the fitness for purpose warranty by the Norwegian suppliers, the third parties:

The scope and application of section 14(1) of the Sale of Goods Act 1893 was fully considered by this House in *Hardwick Game Farm* v. *Suffolk Agricultural Poultry Producers Association Ltd* [1969] 2 A.C. 31. The opinion expressed in that case endorsed a tendency which other cases (such as *Manchester Liners Ltd* v. *Rea Ltd* [1922] 2 A.C. 74) had shown, to expand the scope of section 14(1) so as to cover territory which might otherwise, on a first reading, have been thought to belong to section 14(2). I think that this tendency essentially reflects a reversion to the more general approach to questions of the seller's liability under implied warranty adopted by the common law, as contrasted with the compartmentalisation into separate, but inevitably overlapping, provisions adopted by the Sale of Goods Act. *Naturam expellas furca* is a maxim which tends to apply to codifications. At any rate it is clear that this House in the *Hardwick* case [1969] 2 A.C. 31 accepted that the 'making known' so as to show reliance which the section requires is easily deduced from the nature and circumstances of the sale, and that the word 'particular' means little more than 'stated' or 'defined'. As Lord Pearce said in *Hardwick*, at p. 115: 'There is no need for a buyer formally to "make known" that which is already known': and here there is no doubt that the third parties, through their selling agents C.T. Bowring & Co. Ltd, and also directly, knew what the herring-meal was required for, namely, for inclusion in animal feeding stuffs to be compounded by the buyers, and no special purpose in relation to mink was relied on. The third parties were, moreover, a committee, or co-operative, of manufacturers of herring meal: in this case, whether one speaks of implication or presumption, the conclusion can hardly be otherwise than that of reliance by the buyers to produce a product reasonably fit for the purpose. I observe, indeed, that my noble and learned friend, Lord Guest, who felt difficulty in *Hardwick* as to the application of section 14(1) against persons who were dealers in the market, said that he could well understand, where the sale is by a manufacturer to a customer, that the inference (sc. of reliance) can easily be drawn (p. 106). I agree with Milmo J. that it ought to be drawn in this case.

Then was the purpose, to be used for inclusion in animal feeding stuffs to be compounded by the buyers, a particular purpose? In my opinion, certainly yes. It is true that the purpose was wide, wider even than the purpose accepted as particular in *Hardwick* [*Kendall* v. *Lillico* above] (for compounding into food for cattle and poultry), and, if one leaves aside a possible alternative use as fertiliser, on which there was some indefinite evidence, the purpose so made known covers a large part of the area which would be within section 14(2). But I do not think, as the law has developed, that this can be regarded as an objection or that in accepting a purpose so defined, as a 'particular purpose,' the court is crossing any forbidden line. There remains a distinction between a statement (express or implied) of a particular purpose, though a wide one, with the implied condition (or warranty) which this attracts, and a purchase by description with no purpose stated and the different condition (or warranty) which that attracts. Moreover, width of the purpose is compensated, from the seller's point of view by the dilution of his responsibility: and to hold him liable under an implied warranty of fitness for the purpose of which he has been made aware, wide though this may be, appears as fair as to leave him exposed to the vaguer and less defined standard of merchantability. After all, the seller's liability is, if I may borrow the expression of my noble and learned friend, Lord Morris of Borth-y-Gest, no more than to meet the requirement of a buyer who is saying to him 'that is what I want it for, but I only want to buy if you sell me something that will do.' I think that well expresses the situation here.

The next point is whether, when the meal turned out to be unsuitable for feeding to mink, this was a matter to be treated as within the seller's responsibility. There are two distinct points here: the first is whether feeding to mink was a normal use, within the general purpose of inclusion in animal feeding stuffs: the second is whether, assuming that the seller's implied warranty did not extend beyond that of general suitability for animals, including possibly mink, the buyers were able to show a breach of that warranty.

In my opinion, we must reinstate the judge's conclusion, that feeding to mink was a normal user in 1961 and known as such to the third parties. That the relevant consignment or part of it might be fed to mink was also known to the respondents.

LORD DIPLOCK

The key to both subsections [14(1)-(2)] is reliance – the reasonable reliance of the buyer upon the seller's ability to make or select goods which are reasonably fit for the buyer's purpose coupled with the seller's acceptance of responsibility to do so. The seller has a choice whether or not to accept that responsibility. To enable him to exercise it he must be supplied by the buyer with sufficient information to acquaint him with what he is being relied upon to do and to enable him to appreciate what exercise of skill or judgment is called for in order to make or select goods which will be fit for the purpose for which the buyer requires them.

This consideration in my view, throws light upon two matters arising under section 14. The first is the meaning of 'particular purpose' in subsection (1). The second is the application of the doctrine of 'partial reliance' under both subsection (1) and subsection (2).

To attract the condition to be implied by subsection (1) the buyer must make known the purpose for which he requires the goods with sufficient particularity to enable a reasonable seller, engaged in the business of supplying goods of the kind ordered, to identify the characteristics which the goods need to possess to fit them for that purpose. If all that the buyer does make known to the seller is a range of purposes which do not call for goods possessing identical characteristics and he does not identify the particular purpose or purposes within that range for which he in fact requires the goods, he does not give the seller sufficient information to enable him to make or to select goods possessing a characteristic which is needed to make them fit for any one of those purposes in particular, if the same characteristic either is not needed to make them fit, or makes them unfit, for other purposes within the range.

A 'range of purposes' case thus poses a stark question of legal policy as to whether the seller's responsibility ought to be to supply goods which are fit for at least one of the purposes within the range or to supply goods which are fit for all of those purposes unless he expressly disclaims responsibility for their fitness for any one or more of them. The answer to this question of policy has, in my view, been pre-empted by subsection (2) of section 14 of the Sale of Goods Act 1893.

The commonest way in which a buyer makes known to the seller a range of purposes for which the goods are required is by the description by which he buys them and by nothing more. This is the case that is contemplated by subsection (2). This, as it has been authoritatively construed by the courts, provides that the only condition to be implied as to the responsibility of the seller is that the goods should be reasonably fit for one of the purposes within the range.

To supplement the description by which the goods are bought, or to replace it if they are not bought by description, the buyer may identify with greater precision the purpose for which the goods are required, by making it known to the seller in some other way. This is the case contemplated by subsection (1). He may do this expressly or by implication. At any rate, if he does so expressly he can make it known to the seller that he relies upon the seller to supply goods that are fit for more than one purpose or, indeed, for all possible purposes which lie within a range. But the mere fact that the seller knows that the buyer is engaged in a business in which goods of the description by which they are bought *may* be needed for any one of a number of purposes within the range of those for which goods of that description are normally used, adds nothing to what he might reasonably infer from the fact that the buyer ordered the goods by a description which covers goods fit for a range of purposes, without particularising which of those purposes he requires goods for it. It might be otherwise if the seller knew that the buyer was engaged in a business in which goods of the description by which they were bought were needed for one or more only of the purposes within the whole range.

It would, in my view, conflict with the principle of reliance which underlies section 14(1) and (2) and would be a misuse of a statutory code of this kind, to treat a range of purposes for any one of which the buyer *may* require the goods, on the one hand, as constituting 'the particular purpose for which the goods are required' and so giving rise to an implied condition under subsection (1) that they shall be reasonably fit for all purposes within the range, if the seller's knowledge of the *range* is derived in whole or in part from some circumstance other than the description by which the goods are ordered; and, on the other hand, as giving rise to an implied condition under subsection (2) that the goods need only be fit for one of the purposes within the range, if the seller's knowledge of the *range* is derived solely from the description by which the goods are ordered. So to construe the code would for practical purposes deprive subsection (2) of any effect.

I turn next to 'partial reliance.' The actual words of subsection (1) appear to contemplate two classes of contracts only; one, where the buyer does not rely at all upon the skill or judgment of the seller to see to it that the goods supplied are reasonably fit for a particular purpose; the other where the buyer does so rely and the other requirements of the subsection are satisfied. As a matter of linguistics it is possible to construe the expression 'so as to show that the buyer relies' as referring to a reliance which was only partial, in the sense that the reliance was not the only or even the determinative factor which induced the buyer to enter into the contract. But it is not possible to extract from the language of the subsection any qualification upon the implied undertaking by the seller, if there is such reliance, that the goods supplied by him shall be reasonably fit for the particular purpose for which they are required by the buyer. Yet as a result of technological advances since 1893 there are an increasing number of cases where the preparation of goods fit for a particular purpose calls for the exercise of more than one kind of expertise. The buyer may himself possess one of the kinds of expertise needed but lack another and may choose a seller who has led him to believe that he, the seller, possesses it. The only reliance by the buyer upon the skill or judgment of the seller is that in the preparation or selection of the goods he will exercise that kind of expertise which he has led the buyer reasonably to believe that he possesses. The goods supplied may then be unfit for the particular purpose for which both parties knew they were required, either because of a defect which lay within the sphere of expertise of the seller or because of a defect which lay within the sphere of expertise of the buyer himself.

The way in which the principle of reliance which underlies subsections (1) and (2) should be applied to a more complex contract of this kind, which was not in the immediate contemplation of the draftsman of the code, poses another stark question of legal policy. In large part this decision was made by your Lordships' House in 1934 in the *Cammell Laird* case [1934] A.C. 402. It was there laid down that if the defect in the goods which rendered them unfit for their purpose was due to a characteristic which it lay within the sphere of expertise of the seller to detect and avoid, the responsibility for their unfitness lay with the seller. The ratio leads ineluctably to the corollary that if the defect was due to a characteristic which it lay within the sphere of the expertise of the buyer to detect and avoid, the seller was not contractually responsible for it. It did not attract the implied condition under subsection (1). The field of the seller's undertaking as to the fitness of the goods for the purpose corresponded with the field of the buyer's reliance upon the skill and judgment of the seller.

My Lords, this seems to me to be consistent with common sense and business honesty. It was accepted as the correct principle by both courts below and by all parties to the appeals in this House. But the *Cammell Laird* case leaves open for decision an ancillary question of legal policy which your Lordships are now called upon to decide for the first time. That question is whether, in a case of partial reliance of this kind, once the goods have been proved to be unfit, for the purpose for which they were required the onus lies upon the buyer to prove that the defect was due to a characteristic which it lay within the field of expertise to the seller to detect and avoid; or does it lie upon the seller to prove that the defect was due to a characteristic which lay within the sphere of expertise of the buyer.

I do not think that there is anything in the Sale of Goods Act 1893 or in hitherto accepted law which inhibits your Lordships from deciding this question whichever way commends itself to the majority. The choice depends largely upon one's personal view as to whether the swing of the pendulum since 1893 from caveat emptor to caveat venditor has now gone far enough and ought to be arrested, or whether it should be given a further impetus, albeit a minor one, upon its current course. For my part I would have been in favour of arresting it. But I recognise that a decision to the contrary is simply one of policy and, as it commends itself to the majority of your Lordships, I accept it with good grace as now forming part of the law of contracts for the sale of goods.

Once it is accepted, it is decisive of the first appeal. Hill's sphere of expertise upon which Udall relied in the selection of ingredients for 'King Size' mink food which would be of a quality suitable for use in compound feeding-stuffs for domestic animals and poultry other than mink. The particular purpose, known to both parties, for which Udall required the 'King Size' mink food was as a feeding-stuff for mink. Udall proved that it was unsuitable for that purpose and that its unsuitability was due to the quality of an ingredient, herring meal, selected by Hill. Upon the findings of fact of Milmo J., Hill failed to prove affirmatively that the herring meal was of a quality suitable for use in compound feeding-stuffs for domestic animals and poultry other than mink. Therefore, Udall is entitled to succeed upon his claim for damages for breach of the condition to be implied under section 14(1) of the Sale of Goods Act 1893.

On the other hand, I do not think that the contract between Udall and Hill was one which attracted any implied condition as to merchantable quality under section 14(2) of the Act. The expression 'merchantable quality' in relation to goods implied that at the time of the contract of sale there already exists a market in goods of the kind described from which it is possible to identify a standard of comparison or norm with which the goods should correspond in order to be acceptable to a reasonable buyer of such goods in that market. There was no existing market in 'King Size' mink food. It was an entirely new product in which Hill made plain to Udall he had never dealt before. The contract was for the sale of goods by description; but whether the description was limited to what was stated in Udall's formula as to the ingredients and their proportions or whether it also included a reference to the goods as a feeding-stuff for mink the description was not one of goods in which Hill dealt within the meaning of section 14(2).

To hold the contrary would, in my view, conflict with the principle of reliance which underlies both subsections (1) and (2) of section 14. If the 'King Size' compound had been unsuitable as a feeding-stuff for mink solely because any food compounded in accordance with Udall's formula would have been unsuitable for mink, it would have been unmerchantable for there was no other purpose for which it could be used in commerce. Yet it would be contrary to common sense and business honesty if Hill who had done precisely that which Udall had reasonably relied upon him to do, were liable for a defect in the goods in a respect in which no reliance had been placed upon Hill.

He went on to deal with the claim against the third parties.

My Lords, before coming to the specific provisions of the Sale of Goods Act 1893, I again prefer to start by posing the question: What, if any, responsibility as to the characteristics of the goods to be supplied under the contract would the seller reasonably understand that the buyer believed that he, the seller, was accepting? And in the circumstances of the present appeal that question can be reduced to this: Would the Norwegians' reasonable understanding and Hill's reasonable belief be that the Norwegians were accepting responsibility to deliver Norwegian herring meal which possessed characteristics which made it suitable for inclusion as an ingredient in the diet of mink, as distinguished from other animals?

So stated, as it seems to me, the question answers itself. Hill never let the Norwegians know that he required the herring meal for feeding to mink. They had no reason to suspect that it was required for a use to which it had never previously been put in the country in which it was to be consumed. The fat content provided for in the contract made it unsuitable for the only use of herring meal as a food for mink of which they had any knowledge, namely, in Norway. They were given no opportunity to exercise any skill or judgment in selecting herring meal which would have the special characteristics which would render it suitable as a food for mink as distinguished from other animals.

Question

The majority held that there was a breach of the merchantable quality in both contracts. How does the case differ from *Kendall* v. *Lillico* (above)?

B.S. BROWN & SON LTD v. CRAIKS LTD [1970] 1 All E.R. 823

The appellants ordered cloth from the respondents. They did not inform the respondents of the purpose for which they required it, which was making dresses. The cloth may have been suitable for industrial purposes, but was not suitable for this purpose. The price of the cloth was higher than would normally have been paid for industrial fabric, but not unreasonably so.

LORD REID

It is evident that at the proof the appellants put most weight on their case under s. 14(1), so it is not surprising that the findings of fact with regard to their case under s. 14(2) are not as detailed as one might have desired. Certainly this kind of cloth of the quality delivered was suitable for industrial use, but we do not know why it was not more frequently used for industrial purposes. There is no suggestion in the findings that the respondents, as dealers in goods of that description, ought to have known or even suspected, that these goods were not intended for industrial use.

All the well-known authorities were cited on the proper interpretation of 'merchantable quality'. Some importance was attached to what I said in *Henry Kendall & Sons (a firm)* v. *William Lillico & Sons Ltd* [1968] 2 All E.R. 444, [1968] 3 W.L.R. 110:

> 'If the description is a familiar one, it may be that in practice only one quality of goods answers that description – then that quality and only that quality is merchantable quality. Or it may be that

various qualities of goods are commonly sold under that description – then it is not disputed that the lowest quality commonly so sold is what is meant by merchantable quality; it is commercially saleable under that description.'

I see no reason to alter what I said, but judicial observation can never be regarded as complete definitions; they must be read in light of the facts and issues raised in the particular case. I do not think that it is possible to frame, except in the vaguest terms, a definition of 'merchantable quality' which can apply to every kind of case. In *Kendall* v. *Lillico* no question as to price arose because the evidence showed that, even when all the facts were known, the market price was the same for tainted and untainted goods. But suppose that the market price for the better quality is substantially higher than that for the lower quality. Then it could not be right that, if the contract price is appropriate for the better quality, the seller should be entitled to tender the lower quality and say that, because the lower quality is commercially saleable under the contract description, he has fulfilled his contract by delivering goods of the lower quality. But I think that the evidence in this case with regard to prices is much too indefinite to support a case on that basis.

Illustrations of the application of the quality warranties

NIBLETT LTD v. CONFECTIONERS' MATERIALS CO. LTD [1921] 3 K.B. 387

The condensed milk in this case was of satisfactory quality, but was contained in tins whose label bore a brand name which infringed a registered trade mark. As a result the labels had to be removed and the goods sold at a loss. *Held*: by Bankes and Atkins L.J. (Scrutton L.J. expressing no opinion) that there was a breach of the warranty of merchantability.

For the s. 12 issue see p. 49, above.

BANKES L.J.
I think there is also a cause of action under s. 14, sub-s. 2, because these goods were not 'of merchantable quality'. Quality includes the state or condition of the goods. The state of this condensed milk was that it was packed in tins bearing labels. The labels were as much part of the state or condition of the goods as the tins were. . . The phrase in s. 14, sub-s. 2, is, in my opinion, used as meaning that 'the article is of such quality and in such condition that a reasonable man acting reasonably would after a full examination accept it under the circumstances of the case in performance of his offer to buy that article whether he buys it for his own use or to sell again.' If the warranty that the goods shall be of merchantable quality applies to a complicated machine it applies equally to the packing in which the goods are presented which may, and does in this case, form a most important feature of the goods as delivered.

SUMNER PERMAIN & CO. v. WEBB [1922] 1 K.B. 551

The defendants sold some 'Webbs Indian Tonic Water' to the plaintiffs. The defendants knew it was bought for shipment to Argentina. The tonic water was condemned as unfit for human consumption in Argentina because it contained a prohibited ingredient 'salicylic acid'.

SCRUTTON L.J.

In my view 'merchantable quality' means that the goods comply with the description in the contract, so that to a purchaser buying goods of that description the goods would be good tender. It does not mean that there shall in fact be persons ready to buy the goods. For instance take the case that I put during the argument; if you sell 'vestings' of a particular fancy pattern for sale in China, you do not warrant that the Chinese buyer will like that pattern and will buy it when it goes out there; if the goods are vestings of the pattern contracted for, they are merchantable though nobody likes the pattern or is willing to buy. Similarly I do not think 'merchantable quality' means that there can legally be buyers of that article. If the goods are of the contract description the possibility of legally making a sale of them does not in my view come within the expression 'merchantable quality'. I am still not quite clear when that expression first began to be used. I see that in *Randall* v. *Newson* 2 Q.B.D. 102, 109, Lord Esher (or Brett J.A. as he then was) appears to have thought that it was first used in *Gardiner* v. *Gray* (1815) 4 Camp. 144, 145. There was in that case a count 'that the silk should be waste silk of a good and merchantable quality', and it was in reference to that count that Lord Ellenborough used the language which has repeatedly been quoted in other cases. 'The intention of both parties must be taken to be that it shall be saleable in the market under the denomination mentioned in the contract between them. The purchaser cannot be supposed to buy goods to lay them on a dunghill'; and that particular picturesque passage has been cited by judge after judge in cases on this point ever since. Now when Lord Ellenborough there uses the word 'saleable' I do not think he means 'legally saleable'. As explained by Lord Esher himself in *Randall* v. *Newson* 2 Q.B.D. 102, 109, the fundamental thing is that 'the article offered or delivered shall answer the description of it contained in the contract'. And in a passage a little later on he adds: 'If that subject matter be merely the commercial article or commodity, the undertaking is, that the thing offered or delivered shall answer that description, that is to say, shall be that article or commodity, saleable or merchantable,' or in other words shall be a good tender under a contract for a sale of goods of that description. I am quite unable to find that any case since has ever dealt with the possibility of legally selling the goods in the particular market and has treated that possibility as included in the definition of 'merchantable'. For these reasons I disagree with the view taken by Bailhache J.

TEHERAN-EUROPE CO. LTD v. S.T. BELTON (TRACTORS) LTD [1968] 2 Q.B. 545

The facts are given in Lord Denning's judgement:

LORD DENNING M.R.
Teheran-Europe Ltd is a company incorporated in Persia which carries on business in Teheran. It imports machinery into Persia and resells it there. It buys machinery in England through an intermediary called Richards Marketing Ltd, which is an English company carrying on business in London. In 1957, the managing director of the Persian company came over to England. He was interested in machines called air compressors. Some of these machines were being offered for sale by a company called S.T. Belton (Tractors) Ltd, of Boston, Lincolnshire. That company had acquired several of these compressors as surplus Government stores. Eventually, a contract was made for the purchase of 12 of these air compressors at £340 each. Six of them were delivered. The Persian company complained that they were not up to contract and brought an action against S.T. Belton (Tractors) Ltd for breach of contract. . .

So far as section 14(1) is concerned, it is quite clear that the buyers made known to the sellers that they were required for resale in Persia. In the letter of August 10, 1967, Richards Marketing Ltd wrote to S.T. Belton (Tractors) Ltd: 'We have now received provisional estimates for packing these units singly suitable for shipment to Khorranshahr, and cross-country transit.' Khorranshahr, as far as I understand it, is in Persia. And then in the letter of August 19, 1957 they said: 'Our clients are asking for a liberal supply of descriptive literature for advertising purposes in Iran.' So that is quite clear that the buyers made known to the sellers that they required them for resale in Persia.

But the section of the statute contains a further requirement before a condition is implied. The particular purpose must be made known to the seller so as to show that the buyer relies on the seller's skill and judgment. The judge held that, once the purpose was made known, there was an inference that the buyer relied on the seller's skill and judgment. He quoted some of the speeches in *Manchester Liners Ltd* v. *Rea Ltd* [1922] 2 A.C. 74; 38 T.L.R. 526, H.L.(E). But that case has, in the last few days, been considered by the House of Lords in the *Hardwick Game Farm* v. *Suffolk Agricultural Poultry Producers Association* [1968] 3 W.L.R. 110; [1968] 2 All E.R. 444, H.L.(E.), case. Lord Reid said [1968] 3 W.L.R. 110, 128:

> 'I do not think that this case [*Manchester Liners Ltd* v. *Rea Ltd* [1922] 2 A.C. 74] is any authority for the view which has sometimes been expressed that if the seller knows the purpose for which the buyer wants the goods it will be presumed that the buyer relied on his skill and judgment.'

So the observations in *Manchester Liners Ltd* v. *Rea Ltd* [1922] 2 A.C. 74 have received a knock-out blow. We can revert once more to the statute. The particular purpose must be made known 'so as to show that the buyer relies on the seller's skill or judgment.' That means that the buyer makes the particular purpose known to the seller in such a way that the seller knows that he is being relied upon. That cannot be said here. The sellers did not know they were being relied on for resale in Persia. They knew nothing of conditions in Persia. The buyers knew all about those conditions. The buyers saw the machine here. They read its description. They relied upon their own skill and judgment to see that it was suitable for resale in Persia, and not on the seller's. At all events, they did not make the purpose known to the seller in such circumstances as to show him that they relied on the seller's skill and judgment. So I do not think there was an implied term that they should be fit for the purpose of being resold in Persia. So on this point I differ from the judge and I would allow the appeal accordingly. I say nothing as to how the knowledge might affect the measure of damages; that is a matter which is not before us. I would therefore affirm the judge on the first issue and reverse him on the second.

Question

Consider these cases in the light of Lord Diplock's speech in *Ashington Piggeries Ltd* v. *Christopher Hill Ltd* (above, p. 78). To what extent do you think a similar approach underlies them?

VACWELL ENGINEERING CO. LTD v. B.D.H. CHEMICALS [1969] 3 All E.R. 1681

The defendants contracted to supply boron tribromide to the plaintiffs for use in their manufacturing process. Boron tribromide is highly explosive on contact with water. It was supplied to the plaintiffs in glass ampoules with labels bearing no warning of the danger. While the labels were being washed off, a necessary preliminary to the manufacturing process, a violent explosion occured. Scientific literature from 1897 onwards contained warnings of the danger.

REES J.
I now turn to the issues of law to which the case gives rise, and first to those arising on contract. Vacwell's case in contract is put in two ways: First on s. 14(1) of the Sale of Goods Act 1893. Section 14 is in these terms:

> '. . . (1) Where the buyer, expressly or by implication, makes known to the seller the particular purpose for which the goods are required, so as to show that the buyer relies on the seller's skill or judgment, and the goods are of a description which it is in the course of the seller's business to supply (whether he be the manufacturer or not), there is an implied condition that the goods shall be reasonably fit for such purpose, . . .'

The two essentials which must be established by the buyers are: (i) that they made known to the sellers the particular purpose for which the goods were required; and (ii) that they did so in such a way as to show that they relied on the sellers' skill and judgment. On these questions I was referred to two recent cases of high authority. The first was a decision of the House of Lords. *Henry Kendall & Sons (a firm)* v. *William Lillico & Sons., Ltd*, [1968] 2 All E.R. 444; [1968] 3 WLR 110. This case contains valuable guidance on the construction of this subsection in general, and in particular on that part of it which relates to the necessity for the buyer to establish that he showed that he was relying on the sellers' skill and judgment. I cite two passages from the speech of LORD REID on this aspect of the matter ([1968] 2 All E.R. at p. 453; [1968] 3 WLR at p. 126):

> 'On the face of it s. 14(1) of the Act of 1893 has a narrower scope. It requires that the buyer shall have required the goods for a particular purpose, that that purpose shall have been made known to the seller, and that it shall have been made known to him in such circumstances that he realised or ought to have realised that the buyer was relying on his using his skill or judgment to select goods fit for that purpose. Many cases in which the seller has been held liable under this subsection might equally well and more logically have been decided under s. 14(2); but there has been a tendency to construe sub-s. (2) too narrowly and to compensate for that by giving a wide construction to sub-s. (1).'

In the second passage, LORD REID, referring to *Manchester Liners Ltd* v. *Rea Ltd* [1922] 2 A.C. 74; [1922] All E.R. Rep. 605, said ([1968] 2 All E.R. at p. 455; [1968] 3 W.L.R. at p. 128):

> 'I do not think that this case is any authority for the view, which has sometimes been expressed, that if the seller knows the purpose for which the buyer wants the goods it will be presumed that the buyer relied on his skill and judgment.'

In a recent case there is a helpful comment by LORD DENNING, M.R. on the passage from LORD REID's speech which I have just read; I refer to *Teheran-Europe Co Ltd*, v. *S.T. Belton (Tractors) Ltd*, [1968] 2 All E.R. 886 at p. 890; [1968] 2 A.B. 545 at p. 554, where LORD DENNING, M.R. said this:

> 'So the observation in *Manchester Liners Ltd* v. *Rea Ltd* [1922] 2 A.C. 74; [1922] All E.R. Rep. 605, have received a knock-out blow. We can revert once more to the act of 1893. The particular purpose must be made known "so as to show that the buyer relies on the seller's skill or judgment." That means that the buyer makes the particular purpose known to the seller in such a way that the seller knows that he is being relied on. That cannot be said here.'

With these principles in mind, I turn to the central question in the instant case, namely, have Vacwell shown that, when they ordered boron tribromide from B.D.H., they made known to B.D.H. the particular purpose for which they required that chemical, in such a way as to make B.D.H. realise that they were relying on their skill and judgment? B.D.H. certainly knew that the chemical was required for use in the course of the manufacture of semi-conductor or transistor material; further, as I have found, prior to the contract two representatives of B.D.H. actually saw the equipment used in the process of manufacture. It is equally clear, however, that it was Vacwell who decided to use boron tribromide in the process and did not in fact rely on the skill or judgment of B.D.H. in that decision; nor did they lead B.D.H. to suppose that they had done so. Nevertheless, I am satisfied that, as a result of the course of dealing between the parties up to the date of the contract (be that in February or in April 1966), Vacwell did rely on the skill of B.D.H. to warn them of any unusual hazard which might arise in the ordinary handling and industrial use of a chemical purchased from B.D.H. I draw this inference from the facts that, in purchase of chemicals made by Vacwell from B.D.H. prior to the contract, they had found that each product bought contained a label bearing, where appropriate, a warning notice of an industrial hazard and that such purchase of boron tribromide as Vacwell had made prior to the relevant date (for example, that of November 1965) did contain a warning of a particular hazard. There is an overwhelming inference from the whole of the evidence that 24 of the chemicals ordered by Vacwell from B.D.H. in September 1965 contained a suitable warning label (I omit the 25th item, which I understand is a branded detergent). I also find that it is a reasonable inference to draw in all the circumstances from the nature of the respective businesses of Vacwell and B.D.H. that Vacwell would, and did, rely on B.D.H. to give such a warning.

Do these findings amount to evidence that Vacwell showed B.D.H. that Vacwell relied on the skill and judgment of B.D.H. that the goods were reasonably fit for the purpose of being used in Vacwell's industrial process? The answer to that question is not an easy one. Boron tribromide as such was chosen by Vacwell without any reliance on B.D.H. and it was fit for the purpose in all respects save one, namely, that it was not fit for use in any context in which there was a risk of contact with water. There was in the process actually adopted by Vacwell a risk of contact with water, and without an express warning I find that there was a reasonably foreseeable risk of such contact in the ordinary course of any industrial use to which boron tribromide might be put by a manufacturer. It is also true that an ampoule of boron tribromide, provided it bears the present warning label, is now, and would have been, fit for the purpose of use in the course of an ordinary industrial process. On the whole, I think that the right view is that, in all the circumstances, there was an implied condition of fitness for the purpose arising on this contract.

Next, was there a breach? My findings are that B.D.H. supplied boron tribromide to Vacwell in glass ampoules for use in an industrial process in the ordinary course of which B.D.H. knew would, or might, come into contact with water by accidental breakage of the glass or otherwise, for example as envisaged by Dr. Burgoyne. The result of contact with water was likely to be a violent, and even an explosive, reaction. In my judgment, a breach of the implied term has been established. In this context, it matters not that B.D.H. did not know of the explosion hazard at the relevant time. . . . Vacwell also pleaded reliance on s. 14(2) of the Sale of Goods Act 1893. However, their counsel, while keeping the points open, did not desire to present an argument to me on a breach of this subsection; I do not, therefore, deal with it save to observe that there appear to me to be a number of difficulties in establishing a breach of this provision.

Question

The above cases predate the Supply of Goods (Implied Terms) Act 1973 which introduced the definition of merchantable quality now found in s. 14(6). What difference, if any, would the new definition of 'merchantable quality' make?

Problems

1. B purchased a new car. Shortly after delivery it broke down. There are no less than twenty-eight defects and B purports to reject for breach of the merchantable quality warranty. Is he entitled to do so given that the Consumers' Association has found in sixteen years of testing that new cars are never free from faults?[68]
2. Suppose that the twenty-eight defects of the car were remedied, but after two months' normal running the engine seized up. Would there be a breach of the merchantable quality warranty because the car was not durable? S. 14(6) is phrased in the present tense: 'Goods . . . *are* of merchantable quality . . . if they *are* as fit . . .'[69]

Note

The Law Commission are considering the definition of merchantable quality at the moment – see p. 11 above.

When is a product defective?

The following extract is concerned with the law governing products liability as it has developed in the United States. The analysis is equally pertinent to English law, however, since ultimately the buyer's complaint must be that the goods are defective in some way.

PRODUCT LIABILITY AND THE MEANING OF 'DEFECT', by Page Keeton (1973) 5 St. Mary's Law Jo. 30, 33

Simply stated, the product must be defective as marketed, and it may be defective as marketed for one or the other of at least three reasons: (1) it may have been fabricated or constructed in the sense that the specific product was not at the time of sale by the maker or other seller in the condition that the maker intended it to be; (2) it may have been improperly designed; and (3) purchasers and those who are likely to use the product may have been misinformed or inadequately informed, either about the risks and dangers involved in the use of the product or how to avoid or minimise the harmful consequences from such risks. In so stating, it must be obvious that while different categories of defects are recognized, there has been no resolution of the ultimate question as to the meaning of defect.

Compare Art. 2 of the European Convention on Products Liability in regard to Personal Injury and Death: 'A product has a "defect" when it does not provide the safety which a person is entitled to expect, having regard to all the circumstances including the presentation of the product.'

HEIL v. HEDGES (1951) 1 T.L.R. 512

The defendant, a butcher, sold pork chops to the plaintiff. As a result of eating the chops she became ill with trichinosis.

MCNAIR J.

Continuing, his Lordship said – The next question is whether the defendant was in breach of the implied condition of reasonable fitness and merchantability under section 14(1)[70] and (2)[71] of the Sale of Goods Act, 1893. I have already stated that the evidence satisfies me that if pork infested with *trichinella* is subjected to a temperature of 131 deg. F., or on a more conservative estimate 137 deg. F., the *trichinella* is killed and the port is innocuous. I am also satisfied on the evidence called by the defendant that it is common knowledge among the general public, as distinct from experts in nutrition and dietectics, that pork should be cooked substantially longer than other meat, given the same temperature, and that the proper way to cook pork is to cook until white. A well-qualified witness called by the defendant told me that she had consulted 40 or 50 cookery books on the subject and that they were all to the same effect. She had also by way of reinforcing her view, asked a number of housewives of humble station as to their views, and they had unanimously formed the view which she had formed.

In these circumstances it seems to me that, so far as *trichinella spiralis* is concerned, the implied condition of fitness or merchantability is complied with if the pork, when supplied, is in such condition that if properly cooked according to accepted standards it is innocuous. There is apparently no very precise English authority on this point, and I have accordingly been usefully referred to certain Canadian and American authorities which, on examination, seem to support this view. These authorities were: *Yachetti* v. *John Duff and Sons Ltd*

([1943] 1 D.I.R. 194,) a decision of the Court of first instance in Ontario; *Cheli* v. *Cudahy Brothers* ((1934) 255 N.W. 414); *Feinstein* v. *Daniel Reeves* ((1936) 14 F. Supp. 167). I do not find anything in *McSpendon* v. *Kunz* ((1936) 271 N.Y. 131) which is inconsistent with this view.

It being the common contemplation of the parties that the pork will be cooked before consumption, it seems to me that the implied condition must be applied in relation to pork which is not only cooked but properly cooked according to accepted standards. In my opinion, on the facts, it is plain that the pork in question in this case was not properly cooked according to accepted and known standards, but was fit for human consumption and merchantable if so cooked. Accordingly, in my judgment, the plaintiff's allegation that the implied conditions of fitness and merchantability were broken fails.

WEBSTER v. BLUE SHIP TEA ROOM 198 N.E. 2d 309 (1964)
Supreme Judicial Court of Massachusetts

The plaintiff, Mrs Priscilla Webster, was consuming fish chowder in the defendant's restaurant, when a fish bone lodged in her throat, causing not inconsiderable injury.

REARDON J.
We must decide whether a fish bone lurking in a fish chowder, about the ingredients of which there is no other complaint, constitutes a breach of implied warranty under applicable provisions of the Uniform Commercial Code,[1] the annotations to which are not helpful on this point. As the judge put it in his charge, 'Was the fish chowder fit to be eaten and wholesome? . . . Nobody is claiming that the fish itself wasn't wholesome. . . But the bone of contention here – I don't mean that for a pun – but was this fish bone a foreign substance that made the fish chowder unwholesome or not fit to be eaten. . .'

The defendant asserts that here was a native New Englander eating fish chowder in a 'quaint' Boston dining place where she had been before; that fish chowder, as it is served and enjoyed by New Englanders, 'is a hearty dish, originally designed to satisfy the appetites of our seamen and fishermen'; that this court knows well that we are not talking of some insipid broth as is customarily served to convalescents. We are asked to rule in such fashion that no chef is forced 'to reduce the pieces of fish in the chowder to minuscule size in an effort to ascertain if they contained any pieces of bone.' 'In so ruling,' we are told (in the defendant's brief), 'the court will not only uphold its reputation for legal knowledge and acumen, but will as loyal sons of Massachusetts, save our world-renowned fish chowder from degenerating into an insipid broth containing the mere essence of its former stature as a culinary masterpiece.' Notwithstanding these passionate entreaties we are bound to examine with detachment the nature of fish chowder and what might happen to it under varying interpretations of the Uniform Commercial Code.

Chowder is an ancient dish preexisting even 'the appetites of our seamen and fishermen.' It was perhaps the common ancestor of the 'more refined cream soups, purees, and bisques.' Berolzheimer, *The American Woman's Cook Book* (Publisher's Guild Inc., New York, 1941), p. 176. The word 'chowder' comes from the French 'chaudière', meaning a 'cauldron' or 'pot'. 'In the fishing villages of Britany . . . "faire la chaudière" means to supply a cauldron in which is cooked a mess of fish and biscuit with some savoury condiments, a hodge-podge contributed by the fishermen themselves, each of whom in return receives his share of the prepared dish. The Breton fishermen probably carried the custom to Newfoundland, long famous for its chowder, whence it has spread to Nova Scotia, New Brunswick, and New England.' *A New English Dictionary* (Macmillan and Co., 1893) p. 386. Our literature over the years abound in references not only to the delights of chowder but also to its manufacture. A namesake of the plaintiff, Daniel Webster, had a recipe for fish chowder which has survived into a number of modern cook-books[2] and in which the removal of fish bones is not mentioned at all. One old time recipe recited in the *New English Dictionary* study defines chowder as 'A dish made of fresh fish (esp. cod) or clams, stewed with slices of pork or bacon, onions, and biscuit. Cider and champagne are sometimes added.' Hawthorne, in *The House of the Seven Gables* (Allyn and Bacon, Boston, 1957) p. 8, speaks of 'a codfish of sixty pounds, caught in the bay, which had been dissolved into the rich liquid of a chowder.' A chowder variant, cod 'Muddle,' was made in Plymouth in the 1890s by taking 'a three or four pound codfish, head added. Season with salt and pepper and boil in just enough water to keep from burning. When cooked, add milk and pieces of butter.'[3] The recitation of these ancient formulae suffices to indicate that in the construction of chowders in these parts in other years, worries about fish bones played no role whatsoever. This broad outlook on chowders has persisted in more modern cookbooks. 'The chowder of today is much the same as the old chowder . . .' *The American Woman's Cook Book*, *supra*, p. 176. The all embracing Fannie Farmer states in a portion of her recipe, fish chowder is made with a 'fish skinned, but head and tail left on. Cut off head and tail and remove fish from backbone. Cut fish in 2 inch pieces and set aside. Put head, tail, and backbone broken in pieces, in stewpan; add 2 cups cold water and bring slowly to boiling point. . .' The liquor thus produced from the bones is added to the balance of the chowder. Farmer, *The Boston Cooking School Cook Book* (Little Brown Co., 1937), p. 166.

Thus, we consider a dish which for many long years, if well made, has been made generally as outlined above. It is not too much to say that a person sitting down in New England to consume a good New England fish chowder embarks on a gustatory adventure which may entail the removal of some fish bones from his bowl as he proceeds. We are not inclined to tamper with age old recipes by any amendment reflecting the plaintiff's view of the effect of the Uniform Commercial Code upon them. We are aware of the heavy body of case law involving foreign substances in food, but we sense a strong distinction between them and those relative to unwholesomeness of the food itself, e.g., tainted mackerel (*Smith* v. *Gerrish*, 256 Mass. 183, 152 N.E. 318), and a fish bone in a fish chowder. Certain Massachusetts cooks might cavil at the ingredients contained in the chowder in this case in that it lacked the heartening lift of salt pork. In any event, we consider that the joys of life in New England include the ready availability of fresh fish chowder. We should be prepared to cope with the hazards of fish bones, the occasional presence of which in chowders is, it seems to us, to be anticipated, and which, in the light of a hallowed tradition, do not impair their fitness or merchantability. While we are buoyed up in this conclusion by *Shapiro* v. *Hotel Statler Corp.*, 132 F. Supp. 891 (S.D. Cal.), in which the bone which afflicted the plaintiff appeared in 'Hot Barquette of Seafood Mornay,' we know that the United States District Court of Southern California, situated as are we upon a coast, might be expected to share our views. We are most impressed, however, by *Allen* v. *Grafton*, 170 Ohio St. 249, 164 N.E. 2d 167, where in Ohio, the Mid-west, in a case where the plaintiff was injured by a piece of oyster shell in an order of fried oysters, Mr Justice Taft (now Chief Justice) in a majority opinion held that 'the possible presence of a piece of oyster shell in or attached to an oyster is so well known to anyone who eats oysters that we can say as a matter of law that one who eats oysters can reasonably anticipate and guard against eating such a piece of shell. . .' (P. 259 of 170 Ohio St., p. 174 of 164 N.E. 2d)

Thus, while we sympathize with the plaintiff who has suffered a peculiarly New England injury, the order must be exceptions sustained.

1. '(1) Unless excluded or modified by section 2-316, a warranty that the goods shall be merchantable is implied in a contract for their sale if the seller is a merchant with respect to goods of that kind. Under this section the serving for value of food or drink to be consumed either on the premises or elsewhere is a sale. (2) Goods to be merchantable must at least be such as . . . (c) are fit for the ordinary purposes for which such goods are used . . .', G.L. c. 106, § 2-314.

   . . . (3) (b) [W]hen the buyer before entering into the contract has examined the goods or the sample or model as fully as he desired or has refused to examine the goods there is no implied warranty with regard to defects which an examination ought in the circumstances to have revealed to him. . .' G.L. c.106, § 2-316.
2. 'Take a cod of ten pounds, well cleaned, leaving on the skin. Cut into pieces one and a half pounds thick, preserving the head whole. Take one and a half pounds of clear, fat salt pork, cut in thin slices. Do the same with twelve potatoes. Take the largest pot you have. Try out the pork first, then take out the pieces of pork, leaving in the drippings. Add to that three parts of water, a layer of fish, so as to cover the bottom of the pot; next a layer of potatoes, then two tablespoons of salt, 1 teaspoon of pepper, then the pork, another layer of fish, and the remainder of the potatoes. Fill the pot with water to cover the ingredients. Put over a good fire. Let the chowder boil twenty-five minutes. When this is done have a quart of boiling milk ready, and ten hard crackers split and dipped in cold water. Add milk and crackers. Let the

whole boil five minutes. The chowder is then ready to be first-rate if you have followed the directions. An onion may be added if you like the flavour. . . This chowder [he adds] is suitable for a large fishing party.' Wolcott, *The Yankee Cook Book* (Coward-McMann, Inc., New York City, 1939), p. 9.
3. Atwood, *Receipts for Cooking Fish* (Avery & Doten, Plymouth, 1896) p. 8.

GRIFFITHS v. PETER CONWAY [1939] 1 All E.R. 685

The plaintiff contracted dermatitis from a Harris tweed coat made for her by the defendants. Her skin was abnormally sensitive; a normal person would not have been affected by the cloth. She had not made known her abnormality to the defendants.

SIR WILFRID GREENE M.R.
One or two cases were referred to. The only one which I find it necessary to mention, and that for the purpose of distinguishing it, is *Manchester Liners Ltd*, v. *Rea* [1922] 2 A.C. 74; [1922] All E.R. Rep. 605. That was a case where ship owners ordered from the defendants, who were coal merchants, 500 tons of South Wales coal for the bunkers of their steamship, the *Manchester Importer*. It so happened that, owing to the control of the coal trade that was in existence at that time, the supply of bunkering coal was very much restricted, and the defendants, having secured the right to a cargo through the coal controller, proceeded to supply bunker coal out of that cargo to the plaintiffs in satisfaction of the contract. It so happened that the coal so supplied was not suitable for the bunkering of that steamer, which was a natural draught steamer, and, as a consequence, she was obliged to return to port. The owners sued the coal merchants for damages, and relied upon the Sale of Goods Act, 1893, s. 14(1). It was held by the House of Lords, that, on the facts of the case, the implication of the statutory warranty was not rebutted. The ground on which it was said that it was rebutted was connected with the coal control, which limited the source of supply available to the merchants for the purpose of fulfilling their contract. That was negatived. The important matter for the present purpose is that the House of Lords held that, by ordering bunker coal for that particular steamship, the buyer was making known to the seller the particular purpose for which the coal was required. LORD BUCKMASTER said, at p. 79:

> It then remains to be considered whether in the circumstances there was any warranty that the coal was suitable for the purpose for which it was required. It is plain that the order was expressed for the use of a particular steamship, and it must therefore, be assumed that the respondents knew the nature of her furnaces and the character of the coal she used, for it was this coal they contracted to supply.

Mr Morris relies on that passage, and says that this coat was for the use of a particular individual. However, there is all the difference in the world between a case such as that and a case like the present. Steamships differ in types, and some of them have one kind of furnace and some another, and so forth, and the coal which is suitable for one is not necessarily suitable for another. That was a matter which would be within the knowledge of coal merchants, and coal merchants, when they are asked to supply for a particular steamship, are being told 'that is the steamship for which the coal is required,' and, if they do not choose to ascertain what particular type of coal is suitable for the particular furnaces of that steamship, then so much the worse for them. The mere naming of the particular steamship, having regard to the notorious differences between steamships in matters of this kind, was quite obviously a sufficient making known to the seller of the particular purpose. The case here is entirely different, because we are dealing with something abnormal, unknown, which no seller could assume to exist, and, therefore, in my judgment, that case affords no support whatsoever for Mr Morris's proposition. The judge held that the section did not apply. In my opinion, his judgment was perfectly right, and this appeal must be dismissed with costs.

Problems

1. A drug company market a compound aspirin containing an ingredient to which two per cent of the population are allergic. P purchases a bottle of these from D a chemist. P becomes ill as a result of taking them. Would the chemist be liable? Is it a material fact that the aspirins are within a chemist's sphere of expertise, whereas a tailor is not an expert on dermatitis? Would a grocer's shop selling the aspirins be liable? Refer back to the Wade article (p. 62, above).

   If your answer to this last question is 'yes', to what extent is this answer influenced by your desire to see liability placed ultimately on the manufacturer by the retailer suing up the chain?
2. A cosmetic company market an after-shave lotion containing good quality perfume. It is a fact that many people are allergic to the essential oils contained in good quality perfume. Would a shop selling this be liable to those who suffer an allergic reaction after buying the lotion? Would you be prepared to tolerate more adverse effects in necessary and beneficial goods than in luxuries?

Defects which cannot be avoided

There is a troublesome group of cases where goods may be defective, but the seller cannot in the present state of science guard against the defect. Do we hold the seller liable nevertheless? If we do, we may banish from the market a product whose benefits outweigh the slight risk involved.

BALKOWITSCH v. MINNEAPOLIS WAR MEMORIAL BLOOD BANK 132 N.W. 2d 805 (1965): Supreme Court of Minnesota

The plaintiff contracted hepatitis from a transfusion of blood obtained from the defendant blood bank. Payment for the blood was made directly from the plaintiff to the defendant. On the then state of scientific knowledge, it was impossible to detect the virus in blood provided for transfusion.

MURPHY J.
. . . From these authorities it is apparent that courts have rejected the sales analogy by which liability in blood-transfusion cases might be imposed on the theory of implied warranty. We agree with those courts which hold that the furnishing of blood is more in the nature of a service than in the sale of goods. It is our view that the law expressed in the Perlmutter case applies here.

Plaintiffs seek to distinguish the Perlmutter case on the basis that the defendant here is not a hospital as it was there. But we cannot concede that defendant, which is a nonprofit corporation, should be treated differently than a hospital or that it should be characterized as a commercial business which offers it products for sale in the market place in competition with others for the sole motive of making a profit. The acts performed by the hospital in the Perlmutter case are not so unrelated to those performed by the defendant in the case before us as to justify a different result . . . We find it difficult to give literal application of principles of law designed to impose strict accountability in commercial transactions to a voluntary and charitable activity which serves a humane and public health purpose. The activities involved in the transfusion of whole blood, a component of the living body, from one human being to another may be characterized as sui generis in that the sequence of events involve acts common to legal concepts of both a sale and a service. Moreover, it seems to us that under the facts in the case before us it would be unrealistic to hold that there is an implied warranty as to qualities of fitness of human blood on which no medical or scientific information can be acquired and in respect to which plaintiffs' physician has the same information, knowledge, and experience as the supplier.

Note

In *Perlmutter* v. *Beth David Hospital*[72] it was held that such a contract was not a sale but a contract for services. *Frost* v. *Aylesbury Dairies*[73] involved the sale of milk contaminated with typhoid: at that time there was no practical way of testing for this. It was held that there was a breach of the fitness for purpose warranty. The case is not entirely satisfactory, for it does appear that the defendants warranted their milk free from bacteria.

Questions

1. Consider these cases in the light of s. 14(6). Assuming each to involve a sale of goods, what would the outcome be?
2. Why does it matter whether a contract as in *Perlmutter* is held to be for the supply of services, rather than goods? If goods are transferred should not the warranty liability be the same? See p. 105 below.

The privity problem

DANIELS v. R.W. WHITE & SONS LTD and TARBARD [1938] 4 All E.R. 258

The plaintiffs were husband and wife. The husband bought a bottle of the first defendants' lemonade from the second defendant Mrs Tarbard. The lemonade contained carbolic acid and both were injured. It was found as a fact that the manufacturers had taken reasonable care in their manufacturing process.
Held: (1) The manufacturers were not liable to the plaintiffs in negligence, as duty was not to ensure that goods were perfect but only to take reasonable care.

(2) There was a breach by the retailer of the merchantable quality warranty, but not of the fitness for purpose warranty. Accordingly the husband who had bought the lemonade could recover (but not the wife).

LEWIS J.
I did not stop the case, because I thought that it was right to hear what the defendants had to say. Counsel for the plaintiffs addressed me, and, as he always does, dealt most efficiently with the facts of the case and the evidence. He said that the defendants, upon the hypothesis that they had to rebut any inference of negligence which there might be, had entirely failed to do so. I do not take that view. I have to remember that the duty owed to the consumer, or the ultimate purchaser, by the manufacturer is not to ensure that his goods are perfect. All he has to do is to take reasonable care to see that no injury is done to the consumer or ultimate purchaser. In other words, his duty is to take reasonable care to see that there exists no defect that is likely to cause such injury.

I listened yesterday to a description of the machinery and the method used in these works in dealing with these bottles. The empty bottles are brought in, I dare say, from many parts of London. They are brought, it is true, into the same building and into the same room where the washing and filling of bottles is eventually done. Mr Busse has questioned the propriety of a state of things in which bottles which may come from anywhere, and which may contain poisonous matter, are in the same room in which the washing and the filling takes place. What happens is this. The bottles are brought in. There is a trolley alongside the girl who has to sort out the bottles. It is her duty to look at the bottles and smell them, and, if she finds any bottle with an unpleasant smell, either from poison or from anything else, that bottle is immediately put on the trolley, and at the end of the day is taken away and broken, so as not to be used again. The girl having satisfied herself by her sense of smell and by the general look of the bottle that the bottle is innocuous, it then goes to the washing machine, and there, I am quite satisfied, that bottle has the most thorough washing that any bottle could have. It is washed at least three times. It has a 30-seconds' rinse first of all in hot water. Then it has another rinse in caustic soda at a heat of 130°F. Then it has another rinse in exactly the same process in cold water from the main. The bottles, while this is happening, are inverted – namely, with their necks down – and the washing is done under pressure by a jet. It stands to reason that, if one of these bottles by any chance escapes the nose of the lady who smells it first of all, it is then placed upside down on the carrier which conveys these bottles to the washing, and, if there were half-a-teaspoonful, or, indeed, any amount, of liquid in the bottle, it would of course fall out before the bottle was ever washed at all. During the washing process the bottle is not handled at all, and, when it comes to the end of the carrier washed, the only handling it then receives is to remove it from the carrier and to place it on the machine which fills it. Then it is taken off and the stopper put on.

That method has been described as fool-proof, and it seems to me a little difficult to say that, if people supply a fool-proof method of cleaning, washing and filling bottles, they have not taken all reasonable care to prevent defects in their commodity. The only way in which it might be said that the fool-proof machine was not sufficient was if it could be shown that the people who were working it were so incompetent that they did not give the fool-proof machine a chance. It is pointed out quite rightly by Mr Busse that the question of supervision comes in. If you have 16 girls doing this process with no supervision of their work, of course all kinds of accidents may happen. A bottle may get to the filler without ever having been washed at all. A girl may upset a bottle just after it has been filled. She finds, let us say, that two teaspoonfuls of the liquid have been poured out. She has to fill it up from somewhere, so she walks along to the trolley where the dirty bottles have been put, picks up the first bottle she sees there, and pours the contents into the lemonade. Of course, that would be a rather curious thing for anyone to do, but it is a possible thing to happen if there is no supervision in this process.

I am satisfied in this case that there is supervision. I have had called before me the works manager who has charge of all three factories. That means, of course, that he is not at one factory the whole time, but he has described to me what takes place in this particular factory, and I am satisfied that there is quite adequate supervision. Even if the true view be that there was here a case for the defendants to answer, I am quite satisfied that they have answered it, and that the plaintiffs, as a result, have entirely failed to prove to my satisfaction that the defendant company were guilty of a breach of their duty towards the plaintiffs – namely, a duty to take reasonable care to see that there should be no defect which might injure the plaintiffs. For that reason, I think that the plaintiffs' claim against the first defendants fails. I have not forgotton, as Mr Busse in his argument pointed out, that there was called from this factory nobody who was doing the mixing, and no foreman. I am quite satisfied, however, on the evidence before me, that the work of this factory is carried on under proper supervision, and, therefore, that there has been no failure of the duty owed by the defendant company to the plaintiffs.

To my mind, it is quite clear that she [Mrs Tarbard] is not liable under sect. 14(1) of the Act, because Mr Daniels did not rely upon her skill and judgment at all. He asked for and obtained exactly what he wanted. If a man goes in and asks for a bottle of R. White's lemonade, or somebody's particular brand of beer, he is not relying upon the skill and judgment of the person who serves it to him. In spite of the argument which has been put forward by counsel for the second defendant, I have some difficulty in seeing – particularly in view of the cases which have been cited to me, and more particularly *Morelli* v. *Fitch & Gibbons* [1928] 2 K.B. 636 – why this was not a case of sale by description within the Sale of Goods Act, 1893, s. 14(2). If it is a case of goods sold by description by a seller who deals in goods of that description, there is an implied condition that the goods shall be of merchantable quality. Unfortunately for Mrs Tarbard, through no fault of hers, the goods were not of merchantable quality. It was suggested by Mr Block that there was an opportunity of examination so as to bring the matter within the proviso to sect. 14(2) of the Act, and he cited an authority to me, but I do not think that the authority takes him the length which he would wish it to do. I therefore find that this was a sale by description, and therefore hold – with some regret, because it is rather hard on Mrs Tarbard, who is a perfectly innocent person in the matter – that she is liable for the injury sustained by Mr Daniels through drinking this bottle of lemonade. However, that, as I understand it, is the law, and therefore I think that there must be judgment for Mr Daniels, who is the only person who can recover against Mrs Tarbard.

Note

The old proviso to s. 14(1) whereby in the case of the sale of a specified article under its patent or trade-name no implied condition as to fitness for purpose was implied, is removed from the new section (14(3)). Would there now be a breach of that section in similar circumstances? See Royal Commission on Civil Liability and Compensation for Personal Injury (Pearson Report) 1978: see also Law Commission

No. 82 Cmd. 6831 and Uniform Commercial Code (1978 text 2-318). Pearson recommends that producers should be strictly liable in tort for death and personal injury caused by defective products.

UNIFORM COMMERCIAL CODE (1978 text)

SS. 2-318 Third Party Beneficiaries of Warranties Express or Implied
Alternative A

A seller's warranty whether express or implied extends to any natural person who is in the family or household of his buyer or who is a guest in his home if it is reasonable to expect that such person may use, consume or be affected by the goods and who is injured in person by breach of the warranty. A seller may not exclude or limit the operation of this section.

Alternative B

A seller's warranty whether express or implied extends to any natural person who may reasonably be expected to use, consume or be affected by the goods and who is injured in person by breach of the warranty. A seller may not exclude or limit the operation of this section.

Alternative C

A seller's warranty whether express or implied extends to any person who may reasonably be expected to use, consume or be affected by the goods and who is injured by breach of the warranty. A seller may not exclude or limit the operation of this section with respect to injury to the person of an individual to whom the warranty extends. As amended 1966.

Mrs Daniel's problem was that there was no privity of contract between her and either of the defendants. The privity rule can give rise to some arbitrary distinctions – e.g. you develop food poisoning as a result of a meal at a restaurant. Why should it make a difference whether you pay, or are someone else's guest? See *Lockett* v. *A. & M. Charles* [1938] 4 All E.R. 170. The following extract suggests some devices for circumventing this problem:

PRODUCTS LIABILITY IN A NUTSHELL, by C.G. Gillan (1958) 37 Oregon L.R. 119, 153

The common law still responds to the challenge of finding a way around the obstacle of the contractual theory of warranty. Having disposed of the tort aspect of the privity rule with dynamic concepts of deceit, invitation, and negligence, it has proceeded to attack the contract side of the question with these fictions, subterfuges, and bold strokes:

(1) The retailer is the consumer's agent to buy.[1]
(2) The retailer is the manufacturer's agent to sell.[2]
(3) The retailer assigns his warranty from the manufacturer to the consumer.[3]

(4) The consumer is a third-party beneficiary of the retailer's contract with the manufacturer.[4]
(5) The manufacturer's marketing of the goods is an offer to the consumer to warrant them if he will buy.[5]
(6) The manufacturer makes a unilateral offer to the consumer.[6]
(7) The manufacturer's marketing of the goods is a representation to the consumer that they are fit to buy.[7]
(8) The defendant is unable to overcome the inference of negligence from circumstantial evidence.[8]
(9) There is an irrebuttable 'presumption' of negligence.[9]
(10) A warranty 'runs with the goods' from the manufacturer to the consumer.[10]
(11) The manufacturer's warranty to the retailer 'inures to the consumer's benefit.'[11]
(12) A warranty runs with food from the manufacturer to the consumer, but not with a food container.[12]
(13) Pure-food statutes make the manufacturer a guarantor of his product as to consumers.[13]
(14) Warranty is confused with negligence.[14]
(15) Food cases are a special exception to the privity rule.[15]
(16) The privity rule is repudiated as contrary to public policy.[16]
(17) The privity rule is simply rejected.[17]
(18) The privity rule is simply ignored.[18]
(19) Breach of implied warranty is a tort.[19]
(20) Section 15(1) of the Uniform Sales Act abolishes the privity requirement.[20] [*equivalent to s. 14(3) S.G.A. 1979*]
(21) Section 15(2) of the Uniform Sales Act includes the consumer as a 'buyer'.[21] [*equivalent to s. 14(2) S.G.A. 1979*]
(22) Section 15(2) of the Uniform Sales Act includes the manufacturer as a 'seller'.[22] [*see above*]
(23) Section 15(2) of the Uniform Sales Act extends the implied warranty of fitness for a general purpose to the consumer.[23] [*see above*]
(24) Impleader sidesteps the privity requirement.[24]
(25) Notice and opportunity to defend make adverse findings against the defendant retailer binding on the manufacturer against whom the retailer has a claim over.[25]
(26) The manufacturer's advertising is an express warranty to the consumer.[26]
(27) The manufacturer's advertising is a negligent express representation to the consumer.[27]
(28) The manufacturer's advertising is a deceit.[28]
(29) The manufacturer is estopped from denying that he has made representations to the consumer.[29]

1. *Wisdom* v. *Morris Hardware Co.*, 151 Wash. 86, 274 Pac. 1050 (1929).
2. *Ward Baking Co.* v. *Trizzino*, 27 Ohio App. 475, 161 N.E. 557 (1928).
3. *Madouros* v. *Kansas City Coca Cola Bottling Co.*, 230 Mo. App. 275, 90 S.W. 2d 445 (1936).

4. *Ward Baking Co.* v. *Trizzino*, 27 Ohio App. 475, 616 N.E. 557 (1928).
5. *Timberland Lumber Co.* v. *Climax Mfg Co.*, 61 F.2d 931 (2d Cir. 1932).
6. *Carlill* v. *Carbolic Smoke Ball Co.*, [1893] 1 Q.B. 256.
7. *Davis* v. *Van Camp Packing Co.*, 189 Iowa 775, 176 N.W. 382 (1920).
8. See DICKERSON, PRODUCTS LIABILITY AND THE FOOD CONSUMER 129-31 (1951), and cases there cited.
9. *Crigger* v. *Coca Cola Bottling Co.*, 132 Tenn. 545, 179 S.W. 155 (1915).
10. *Coca Cola Bottling Works* v. *Lyons*, 145 Miss. 876, 111 So. 305 (1927).
11. *Klein* v. *Duchess Sandwich Co.*, 14 Cal. 2d 272, 93 P.2d 799 (1939).
12. *Escola* v. *Coca Cola Bottling Co.*, 24 Cal. 2d 453, 150 P.2d 436 (1944).
13. *Hunter v. Derby Foods*, 110 F.2d 970 (2d Cir. 1940); PROSSER, TORTS 693 (1st ed. 1941).
14. *Hertzler* v. *Manshum*, 228 Mich. 416, 200 N.W. 155 (1924); *Ward* v. *Morehead City Sea Food Co.*, 171 N.C. 33, 87 S.E. 958 (1916).
15. *Hertzler* v. *Manshum*, *supra* note 14; *Mazetti* v. *Armour and Co.*, 75 Wash. 622, 135 Pac. 633 (1913).
16. *Williams* v. *Campbell Soup Co.*, 80 F. Supp. 865 (W. D. Mo. 1948).
17. DICKERSON, PRODUCTS LIABILITY AND THE FOOD CONSUMER 96 (1951), and cases cited in n.7.
18. Ibid.
19. See id at 100-1.
20. *Klein* v. *Duchess Sandwich Co.*, 14 Cal. 2d 272, 93 P. 2d 799 (1939).
21. See DICKERSON, PRODUCTS LIABILITY AND THE FOOD CONSUMER 105-6 (1951).
22. Schneider, *Effect of Advertising on the Manufacturer's Liability*, 22 WASH, U.L.Q. 406 (1937).
23. See DICKERSON, PRODUCTS LIABILITY AND THE FOOD CONSUMER 107 (1951).
24. *Cohen* v. *Dugan Bros.*, 134 Misc. 155, 235 N.Y. Supp. 118 (Sup. Ct. 1929).
25. *Carleton* v. *Lombard, Ayres and Co.*, 149 N.Y. 137, 43 N.E. 422 (1896).
26. *Baxter* v. *Ford Motor Co.*, 168 Wash. 456, 12 P.2d 409 (1932).
27. DICKERSON, PRODUCTS LIABILITY AND THE FOOD CONSUMER 133 n.2 (1951).
28. *Baxter* v. *Ford Motor Co.*, 168 Wash. 456, 12 P.2d 409 (1932).
29. Steensland, *Liability of the Manufacturer to the Ultimate Consumer Under Modern Merchandising Practices*, 9 MONT. L. REV. 101, 107 (1948).

Where does the buck stop?

Were we to abandon the privity doctrine, and allow suits to be brought for breach of the Sale of Goods quality warranties, directly against manufacturers, we might ultimately find ourselves driven to draw an artificial line to protect some parties in the chain. Many modern products are manufactured from components, the makers of which may be in a very small way, and unable to insure or otherwise spread the potential loss their products may cause. Holding them liable may cause the particular component to go off the market, and yet it may be essential. The following case illustrates this problem very well (and bear in mind that the same problem could arise in England at the present time if each seller sued back down the line).

GOLDBERG v. KOLLSMAN INSTRUMENT CORP. (1963) 191 N.E. 2d. 81

DESMOND C.J.

The suit is by an administratrix for damages for the death of her daughter-intestate as the result of injuries suffered in the crash near La Guardia Airport, New York City, of an airplane in which the daughter was a fare-paying passenger on a flight from Chicago to New York. American Airlines, Inc., owner and operator of the plane, is sued here for negligence (with present respondents Lockheed and Kollsman) but that cause of action is not the subject of this appeal. The two causes of action, from the dismissal of which for insufficiency plaintiff appeals to us, run against Kollsman Instrument Corporation, manufacturer or supplier of the plane' altimeter, and Lockheed Aircraft Corporation, maker of the plane itself. Kollsman and Lockheed are charged with breaching their respective implied warranties of merchantability and fitness. Those breaches, it is alleged, caused the fatal crash.

There is nothing in the complaint that says where the plane or its altimeter were manufactured or sold nor does the pleading inform us as to decedent's place of residence, although it is alleged that plaintiff's appointment as administratrix was by a New York court. Plaintiff argues that California law should apply on the 'grouping of contracts' theory and it is clear (indeed in effect conceded by respondents) that California law allows recovery for a proven breach of implied warranties as to dangerous instrumentalities (see *Peterson* v. *Lamb Rubber Co.*, 54 Cal. 2d 339, 347, 5 Cal.Rptr. 863, 353 P.2d 575; *Greenman* v. *Yuba Power Prods., Inc.*, 59 Cal.2d 67, 27 Cal.Rptr. 697, 377 P.2d 897). Special Term, however, said in its opinion in the present case that the governing law is that of New York State where the accident took place, citing *Poplar* v. *Bourgois, Inc.*, 298 N.Y. 62, 80 N.E. 2d 334 and that under New York law no claim for breach of implied warranty may be enforced by one not in privity with the warrantor. The Appellate Division, affirming, wrote no opinion. The Special Term opinion, as we have said above, was filed before our Greenberg and Randy Knitwear decisions (*supra*) and Greenberg and Randy Knitwear declared that in New York privity of contract is not always a requisite for breach of warranty recoveries. The Randy Knitwear opinion (11 N.Y. 2d p. 16, 226 N.Y.S.2d p. 370, 181 N.E.2d p. 404) at least suggested that all requirements of privity have been dispensed with in our State. That is the immediate, or at least the logical and necessary result of our decisions and, accordingly, it really makes no difference whether New York or California law be applied, since in this respect both States use the same rules.

The enormous literature on this subject and the historical development of the law of warranties to its present state need not be reviewed beyond the references in our Greenberg and Randy Knitwear opinions (*supra*). A breach of warranty, it is now clear, is not only a violation of the sales contract out of which the warranty arises but is a tortious wrong suable by a noncontracting party whose use of the warranted article is within the reasonable contemplation of the vendor or manufacturer. As to foodstuffs we definitively ruled in *Greenberg* v. *Lorenz*, 9 N.Y.2d 195, *supra*, 213 N.Y.S.2d 39, 173 N.E.2d 773, that the persons thus protected and eligible to sue include the purchaser's family. We went no further in that case because the facts required no farther reach of the rule.

The concept that as to 'things of danger' the manufacturer must answer to intended users for faulty design or manufacture is an old one in this State. The most famous decision is *MacPherson* v. *Buick Motor Co.*, 217 N.Y. 382, 111 N.E. 1050, L.R.A. 1916F, 696, holding the manufacturer liable in negligence to one who purchased a faulty Buick automobile from a dealer . . . But the MacPherson opinion cites much older cases such as *Devlin* v. *Smith*, 89 N.Y. 470 (1882), where one who negligently built a scaffold for a contractor was adjudged liable to the contractor's injured employee. MacPherson and its successors dispelled the idea that a manufacturer was immune from liability in tort for violation of his duty to make his manufacturers fit and safe. In MacPherson's day enforcement required a suit in negligence. Today, we know from *Greenberg* v. *Lorenz*; *Randy Knitwear, Inc.* v. *American Cyanamid Co.* (*supra*) and many another decisions in this and other States . . . that, at least where an article is of such a character that when used for the purpose for which it is made it is likely to be a source of danger to several or many people if not properly designed and fashioned, the manufacturer as well as the vendor is liable, for breach of law-implied warranties, to the persons whose use is contemplated. The MacPherson holding was an 'extension' of existing court-made liability law. In a sense, *Greenberg* v. *Lorenz* and *Randy Knitwear, Inc.* v. *American Cyanamid Co.* (*supra*) were extensions in favour of non-contracting consumers. But it is no extension at all to include airplanes and the passengers for whose use they are built – and, indeed, decisions are at hand which have upheld complaints, sounding in breach of warranty, against manufacturers of aircraft where passengers lost their lives when the planes crashed. . . .

As we all know, a number of courts outside New York State have for the best of reasons dispensed with the privity requirement (see Jaeger, *Privity of Warranty: Has the Tocsin Sounded?* 1 Duquesne U.L.Rev.1). Very recently the Supreme Court of California (*Greenman* v. *Yuba Power Prods., Inc.*, 59 Cal.2d Cal.Rptr. 697, 377 P.2d 897 (1963), *supra*) in a unanimous opinion imposed 'strict tort liability' (surely a more accurate phrase) regardless of privity on a manufacturer in a case where a power tool threw a piece of wood at a user who was not the purchaser. The California court said that the purpose of such a holding is to see to it that the costs of injuries resulting from defective products are borne by the manufacturers who put the products on the market rather than by injured persons who are powerless to protect themselves and that implicit in putting such articles on the market are representations that they will safely do the job for which they were built. However, for the present at least we do not think it necessary so to extend this rule as to hold liable the manufacturer (defendant Kollsman) of a component part. Adequate protection is provided for the passengers by casting in liability the airplane manufacturer which put into the market the completed aircraft.

The judgment appealed from should be modified, without costs, so as to provide for the dismissal of the third (Kollsman) cause of action only and, as so modified, affirmed.

(2) SUPPLIERS' LIABILITY IN CONTRACTS FOR THE SUPPLY OF GOODS TO ANALOGOUS SALE

YOUNG & MARTEN LTD v. McMANUS CHILDS LTD [1969] 1 A.C. 454 (H.L.)

Sub-contractors, the appellants Young & Marten Ltd, agreed with the respondent builders to roof certain houses with particular tiles. The work was duly carried out, but the tiles had been defectively manufactured and cracked in frosty weather.

LORD REID

This is a contract for the supply of work and materials and this case raises a general question as to the nature and extent of the warranties which the law implies in such a contract. As regards the contractor's liability for the work done there is no dispute in this case: admittedly it must be done with all proper skill and care. The question at issue relates to his liability in respect of material supplied by him under the contract. The appellants maintain that the warranty in respect of materials is similar to that in respect of work, so that, if the selection of material and of the person to supply it is left to the contractor, he must exercise due skill and care in choosing the material and the person to supply it. But where, as in this case, the material and the supplier were chosen by the respondents, the appellants maintain that there was no warranty as to the fitness or quality of the tiles. The respondents admit that, if it is held that the choice of this type of tile was theirs and theirs alone, there can be no implied warranty that this type of tile was fit for the contract purpose. But they say that there still was a warranty that the tiles would be of good quality and that that warranty must be implied, notwithstanding the fact that they left no choice to the appellants in selecting the person who was to supply the tiles. If that is right, then the respondents must succeed. The loss was not caused by Somerset 13 tiles being unsuitable for the contract purpose: it was caused by the tiles which were supplied being of defective quality.

There is not very much authority on this matter, so it may be well first to consider it as a question of principle. In my view, no warranty ought to be implied in a contract unless it is in all the circumstances reasonable. If authority be required for that proposition I find it in the judgment of the Exchequer Chamber in *Readhead* v. *Midland Railway Co.* (1869) L.R. 4 Q.B. 379, 392:

> 'Warranties implied by law are for the most part founded on the presumed intention of the parties, and ought certainly to be founded on reason, and with a just regard to the interests of the party who is supposed to give the warranty, as well as of the party to whom it is supposed to be given.'

I take first the general question of the contractor's liability where the material which he is required to use can be obtained from any one of several suppliers and the choice of suppliers is left to him. There is no doubt that in every case he is bound to make a proper inspection of the material before using it, and he will be liable if the loss is caused by the use of material which reasonable inspection would have shown to be defective. The question is whether he warrants the material against latent defects.

There are, in my view, good reasons for implying such a warranty if it is not excluded by the terms of the contract. If the contractor's employer suffers loss by reason of the emergence of the latent defect, he will generally have no redress if he cannot recover damages from the contractor. But, if he can recover damages, the contractor will generally not have to bear the loss: he will have bought the defective material from a seller who will be liable under section 14(2) of the Sale of Goods Act, 1893, because the material was not of merchantable quality. And, if that seller had in turn bought from someone else, there will again be liability, so that there will be a chain of liability from the employer who suffers the damage back to the author of the defect. Of course, the chain may be broken because the contractor (or an earlier buyer) may have agreed to enter into a contract under which his supplier excluded or limited his ordinary liability under the Sale of Goods Act. But in general that has nothing to do with the employer and should not deprive him of his remedy. If the contractor chooses to buy on such terms, he takes the risk of having to bear the loss himself if the goods prove to be defective.

Moreover, many contracts for work and materials closely resemble contracts of sale: where the employer contracts for the supply and installation of a machine or other article, the supply of the machine may be the main element and the work of installation be a comparatively small matter. If the employer had bought the article and installed it himself, he would have had a warranty under section 14(2), and it would be strange that the fact that the seller also agreed to instal it should make all the difference.

The specialty in the present case is that these tiles were only made by one manufacturer. So the contractor had to buy them from him or from someone who bought from him. Why should that make any difference? It would make a difference if that manufacturer was only willing to sell on terms which excluded or limited his ordinary liability under the Sale of Goods Act, and that fact was known to the employer and the contractor when they made their contract. For it would be unreasonable to put on the contractor a liability for latent defects when the employer had chosen the supplier with knowledge that the contractor could not have recourse against him. If the manufacturer's disclaimer of liability caused him to supply the goods at a cheaper price, as in theory at least it should, the employer ought not to get the benefit of a cheap price as well as a warranty from the contractor.

A more difficult case would be where the employer and contractor had no reason to suppose, when they made their contract, that the manufacturer would refuse to sell subject to a seller's ordinary liabilities in respect of the goods which he sells. But I need not consider that case now because there is no suggestion that Brownes had refused to sell except on terms which limited their ordinary liability in respect of latent defects in their tiles. No doubt there will be some cases where, although the contractor had a right of recourse against the manufacturer, he cannot in fact operate that right. The supplier may have become insolvent, or, as in the present case, the action against the contractor may be so delayed that he has no time left in which to sue his supplier. But these cases must be relatively few and it would seem better that the contractor should occasionally have to suffer than that the employer should very seldom have any remedy at all. It therefore seems to me that general principles point strongly to there being an implied warranty of quality in this case.

There is little assistance to be got from the earlier authorities. The first which must be examined is *G.H. Myers & Co.* v. *Brent Cross Service Co.* [1934] 1 K.B. 46. There Myers engaged Brent Cross to repair their motor-car. It was necessary to fit new connecting rods and Brent Cross obtained them from the makers of the car. One had a latent defect so that when the car was used again it broke and caused extensive damage. After reviewing the authorities du Parcq J. said:

> 'I think that the true view is that a person contracting to do work and supply material warrants that the materials which he uses will be of good quality and reasonably fit for the purpose for which he is using them, unless the circumstances of the contract are such as to exclude any such warranty.'

The only addition which I would make is that there are really two warranties, one as to quality and one as to reasonable fitness for the job; and the fact that the latter is excluded, as it is in this case, does not affect the warranty of quality. But I do not think that the example which follows that statement of principle is happily chosen. Whatever may have been the case in 1933, today cases must be rare where the car owner can reasonably suppose that spare parts can be obtained from any other source than the makers of the car. And it may well be that the owner ought at least to suspect that the makers will refuse to supply spare parts without limiting their liability for damage caused by latent defects. So it may well be that this is a case where the circumstances do exclude any warranty by the garage of the quality of the spare parts fitted in repairing the car. It appears to me that less cogent circumstances may be sufficient to exclude an implied warranty of quality where the use of spare parts is only incidental to what is in essence a repairing operation where the customer's main reliance is on the skill of the tradesman, than in a case where the main element is the supply of an article, the installation being merely incidental.

I have had in mind in formulating my opinion the circumstances in *Gloucestershire County Council* v. *Richardson* [1967] 2 All E.R. 458 and the arguments addressed to your Lordships in that case. I do not think it necessary to examine in detail any of the other authorities which have been cited. In the present case one must sympathise with the appellants because, through no fault of their own, they have lost their right of ultimate recourse against the makers of these tiles. But, putting that aside, because the existence or non-existence of the warranty must be determined as at the date of the contract, this appears to me to be a clear case in which a warranty of quality must be implied. I would therefore dismiss this appeal.

LAW COMMISSION WORKING PAPER NO. 71 IMPLIED TERMS IN CONTRACTS FOR THE SUPPLY OF GOODS Part V Provisional Conclusions

We now set out a summary of our main provisional conclusions and recommendations. They are not final views but are intended as a basis for discussion. Comments and criticisms are invited.

Generally

(a) It is desirable that the obligations of the supplier in respect of the goods supplied should be, as nearly as possible, the same, whatever kind of contract (sale, barter, hire, hire-purchase etc.) is employed (paras. 1-16).

Contracts of supply analogous to sale

(b) Where goods are supplied under a contract of barter or under a contract for work and materials, terms as to title, correspondence with description, merchantability, fitness for any particular purpose made known to the supplier and correspondence with sample may be implied (paras. 17-32). However the extent of the obligations is uncertain (paras. 33-36).

(c) The implied obligations of the supplier in respect of goods supplied under a contract of barter or work and materials should be assimilated to those implied in a contract of sale (paras. 37-38).

Contracts of hire

(d) Where goods are supplied under a contract of hire, terms as to quiet possession, correspondence with description, fitness for purpose and correspondence with sample may be implied but they lack clarity in their present form; in particular, there is no doubt as to the nature and extent of the obligation of the supplier to supply goods that are

fit for the purpose of which they are being hired (paras. 39-58).
(e) Subject to the qualifications set out below, the implied obligations of the supplier in respect of goods supplied under a contract of hire should be assimilated to those implied in a contract of sale (paras. 59-64).
(f) As for the implied undertakings regarding the supplier's title and the hirer's right to quiet possession, the following terms should be implied:

(a) the supplier has the right to hire out the goods throughout the period of hire;
(b) the goods are free and will remain free, throughout the period of hire, from any charge or encumbrance not disclosed to the hirer before the agreement was made; and
(c) the hirer is entitled to quiet possession of the goods throughout the period of hire (para. 65)

(g) It is for consideration whether terms as to merchantability or as to fitness for any particular purpose made known to the supplier should be implied in a contract of hire where the goods are supplied otherwise than in the course of a business (paras. 66-68).

Additional terms in contracts of supply
(h) It is for consideration whether additional terms should be implied in contracts of supply (including sale and hire-purchase) in respect of, for example, the durability of the goods, the availability of spare parts and the maintenance of facilities for service and repair (paras. 69-78).

Note

These conclusions deal only with implied obligations equivalent to ss. 12-15, Sale of Goods Act. To what extent do you think that other provisions of the Act might be applicable to contracts for the supply of goods which are not sales, e.g. the risk provisions ss. 16-20, or remedies provisions contained in ss. 49-54?

In contracts of hire one approach has been to hold the supplier liable only for failing to supply goods as fit as reasonable care and skill can make them.[74] To what extent does this standard differ from that expected of a seller under the Sale of Goods Act?

6 Remedies

INTRODUCTION

The mutual expectations of the parties under a contract of sale are (1) on the part of the buyer that he will acquire title to conforming goods in due time, and (2) on the part of the seller that the buyer will duly pay the price. Where the seller becomes entitled to claim the price from the buyer (s. 49), his whole 'expectation interest'[75] is thereby protected: moreover he has a number of expeditious 'real remedies' such as his lien over the goods to secure payment. By contrast, the buyer is not so well served. The equivalent of the seller's action for the price would be an order for specific delivery of conforming goods. In practice this is very seldom awarded. The buyer's remedy for defective performance is characteristically damages. The provisions governing the award of damages to buyers and sellers were derived almost entirely from commercial cases. The expectation interest they protect (albeit imperfectly), is that of the market. The market may not, however, truly represent a consumer's interest under a contract of sale. He may well have an interest in the particular goods over and above that represented by the difference between the contract price and the market price. Economists call this 'consumer surplus'.

CONTRACT REMEDIES AND THE CONSUMER SURPLUS by David Harris, Anthony Ogus and Jennifer Phillips (Centre for Socio-Legal Studies, Oxford), Working Paper No. 1

The Assessment of Damages for Loss of Consumer Surplus (Whether at Common Law or Equity)[1]

Although economics can elucidate the concept of consumer surplus it can offer little guidance on the methods by which a third party, such as a court, could assess in money the value of a lost consumer surplus. Once the contract has been broken, and the parties have been unable to negotiate any settlement of the promisee's claim for the breach, the resolution of the dispute passes to the hands of a third party (whether an arbitrator or judge). The third party is concerned to apply objective legal standards in order to impose a solution on the parties, and in this situation it is undesirable to give the promisee a decisive voice in fixing his own 'price' because he obviously has an incentive to

DOI: 10.4324/9781003174615-7

inflate it. Nevertheless, the judge can, by using the 'reasonable man' approach found in many common law rules, attempt to value the lost consumer surplus: what value would the reasonable man in the promisee's position have put on the consumer surplus which he reasonably expected from performance of this promise? The plaintiff could adduce evidence to show the factors relevant to his expectation of a consumer surplus (e.g. that he was a private collector of rare vases and needed this one to complete a series) which the court could take into account, provided that the defendant either knew of them (or ought, as a reasonable man, to have known of them) at the time of making the contract. The fact that the loss is not quantifiable by reference to a readily-available independent measure (like a market price) should not deter the court[2]: for instance an actor, wrongfully dismissed from a play, may be awared damages for the loss of opportunity to maintain or improve his professional reputation.[3]

The closest approach to the economist's concept of consumer surplus is found in cases where the plaintiff has been wrongfully deprived of an amenity attached to the beneficial use of land.[4] Thus, where the defendant broke a covenant not to develop land for building purposes except in strict accordance with a plan approved by the plaintiffs[5], but the judge decided not to grant an injunction for the demolition of the houses erected in breach of the covenant[6], he concluded that 'a just substitute for a mandatory injunction would be such a sum of money as might reasonably have been demanded by the plaintiffs from [the defendant] as a quid pro quo for relaxing the covenant'.[7] In another case, which was concerned with the use of a right of way for a purpose not envisaged by the original grant, the court fixed the damages at the 'proper and fair price' which the plaintiffs, 'albeit reluctantly', would have been willing to accept for granting the more extensive right of way, viz. 'as compensating them for loss of amenity and increased user.'[8] In the case of the vendor's breach of a contract to sell a house to the defendant for the purpose of his own occupation, a convenient approach would be to fix a percentage[9] of the agreed price as damages for loss of the purchaser's expected consumer surplus.[10]

A second approach to the assessment of damages would be for the court to fix an arbitrary sum to provide some utility to replace that lost by the breach of contract. In personal injury cases, the injured persons's own subjective valuation of his loss utility is ignored, and the courts have fixed arbitrary, conventional sums to compensate for the loss of part of the body, for pain and suffering, or for reduction in the expectation of life.[11] In other situations, the courts have not shrunk from fixing sums to compensate for speculative losses, such as where the breach of contract deprived the promisee of the opportunity to compete for a prize in a beauty contest.[12] The arbitrary sum approach has already been adopted in the holiday cases, where, for instance, breach of a contract to provide an attractive winter sports holiday priced at £63 was met by an award of £125 damages for disappointment and distress at the loss of the promised entertainment and facilities for enjoyment.[13]

A further aspect of damages concerns a sum fixed by the contract as the compensation to be paid for a specified breach of contract. If the sum is a genuine pre-estimate of the loss which the parties (at the time of contracting) expected to flow from the breach, the court will enforce payment of the sum.

In applying this rule, the courts should be willing to treat as part of the expected 'loss' any consumer surplus which the promisee expected to gain from performance of the promise. (The rules on remoteness of damage need not apply, as there is authority for the proposition that losses which might not be covered by the remoteness rules can nevertheless be taken into account when assessing expected losses to justify the sum fixed as liquidated damages.[14])

1. This section excludes consideration where the court fixes the damages at the cost of substitute performance.
2. 'Where precise evidence is obtainable, the court naturally expects to have it, but where it is not, the court must do the best it can' (*Biggin* v. *Permanite Ltd* [1951] 1 K.B. 422, 438); 'As much certainty and particularity must be insisted on, both in pleading and proof of damage, as is reasonable, having regard to the circumstances . . .' (*Ratcliffe* v. *Evans* [1892] 2 Q.B. 524, 532-533) (general loss of business custom in a case of injurious falsehood).
3. *Marbe* v. *George Edwards* [1928] 1 K.B. 269; *Clayton* v. *Oliver* [1930] A.C. 209. Cf. *Withers* v. *General Theatre Corporation* [1933] 2 K.B. 536.
4. Cf. commercial situations, where the defendant has made unauthorised use of the plaintiff's property; the damages have often been fixed at the 'reasonable' rent or hire which the plaintiff could have demanded in a voluntarily negotiated contractual right to use it: *Whitwham* v. *Westminster Brymbo Coal and Coke Co.* [1896] 2 Ch. 538; *Strand Electric and Engineering Co. Ltd*, v. *Brisford Entertainments Ltd* [1952] 2 Q.B. 246; *Penarth Dock Engineering Co. Ltd* v. *Pounds* [1963] 1 Lloyd's Rep. 359.
5. *Wrotham Park Estate Co. Ltd* v. *Parkside Homes Ltd* [1974] 1 W.L.R. 798.
6. 'It would . . . be an unpardonable waste of much needed houses to direct that they now be pulled down' (Ibid., at p. 811).
7. Ibid., at p. 815. On the facts, the judge held that the reasonable man would have required a percentage of the profits which the developer expected to make, and he fixed it on a 'fair' basis at 5% (pp. 815-16).
8. *Bracewell* v. *Appelby* [1975] Ch. 408, 419-20.
9. Cf. the percentage fixed in *Wrotham Park Estate Co. Ltd.* v. *Parkside Homes Ltd.*, *supra* (see note 5, *supra*). In commercial sales of goods, damages for defects have sometimes been fixed as a 'price allowance' or percentage of the price (*Biggin & Co. Ltd.* v. *Permanite Ltd* [1951] 1 K.B. 422, 439).
10. However, since the value to the individual of the consumer surplus of a particular item may depend on the proportion it bears to his total holding of wealth (the poorer man expecting to receive greater utility from a given promise than a richer man), it might be fairer to assess damages for loss of consumer surplus by reference to a percentage of the plaintiff's total holding of wealth; but, in practice, the law could hardly take account of this.
11. Ogus, 35 M.L.R. 1.
12. *Chaplin* v. *Hicks* [1911] 2 K.B. 786.
13 *Jarvis* v. *Swans Tours Ltd.* [1973] Q.B. 233. (The £125 apparently included the cost of the holiday, which the plaintiff had specifically claimed.)
14. *Robert Stewart & Sons Ltd.* v. *Carapanayoti & Co. Ltd.* [1962] 1 W.L.R. 34.

Question

Were consumer surplus generally to be protected, the effect might be that the cost of this would be distributed among other consumers by the supplier raising the price of his goods generally. How would you justify making all of his other customers pay for the subjective expectations of any particular customer?

(1) DISCHARGE BY BREACH

People make bad bargains. Where the market rises after the contract, there is an incentive for the seller to seize on trivial breaches by the buyer as a means of escaping from the contract. Where the market falls the buyer may seek to do likewise. The way in which the law has attempted to deal with this problem is a central theme of this section.

(a) Anticipatory breach

Before the time of performance has arrived, one or other of the parties may repudiate. Ever since the case of *Hochster* v. *De la Tour*[76] the rule has been that the 'innocent' party after such repudiation has an option: either he can 'accept' the repudiation and sue for damages forthwith, or he can 'reject' it, in which case the contract remains in being. The first problem with anticipatory repudiation in the case of contracts for the sale of goods is that the Act appears to render the innocent party's election irrelevant as regards fixing the quantum of damages – see ss. 50(3) and 51(3). This problem is dealt with in the following case.

TAI HING COTTON v. KAMSING KNITTING [1978] A.C. 91 (P.C.)

The defendants agreed to sell to the buyers 1500 bales of cotton at H.K. $1,335 per bale, the buyers to have the right to call for delivery in such instalments as they might demand on giving one month's notice. From late 1971, the sellers failed to supply all the yarn requested and in July 1973 the buyers wrote to the sellers complaining about their delivery record. The sellers replied on 31 July stating that they were treating the contract as repudiated. The buyers declined to accept this repudiation. On 28 November, after unsuccessful attempts to put pressure on the sellers to perform, the buyers issued a writ claiming damages for breach. At the time 424 bales remained undelivered. Were the damages to be assessed at 31 July, the date of refusal to deliver, or 28 December (28 November the date of issue of the writ being the last date on which the buyers could have given one month's notice calling for delivery)?

The judgment of their Lordships was delivered by Lord Keith of Kinkel:

The force of Mr Gatehouse's argument resides essentially in the plain terms of the second limb of section 51(3) [i.e. that damages should be fixed at the time of refusal to deliver.] Their Lordships are attracted by the consideration that this may have been enacted in order to provide a universal rule of simple application for cases where the contract fixes no time for delivery, as where delivery is to be within a reasonable time or on demand by the purchaser. In such cases there may be great difficulty in determining when the contract ought to have been performed, and there could be much convenience in assessing damages as at the date of repudiation by the seller, assuming the buyer accepts it. Further, if the enactment is not intended to apply to a repudiation in such cases, it is difficult to see what content it can have. It could not apply, in cases where delivery is to be made on demand by the buyer, to a refusal to deliver following on a demand duly made, because the demand, having been made in accordance with the contract, would fix the time for delivery. It might be intended to apply, where delivery is to be made within a reasonable time, to a refusal to deliver intimated at the expiry of the period of reasonable time, but if so nothing significant would have been added to the first limb. It may well be, however, that the enactment was introduced into the subsection without consideration in depth of the juristic position, and that on analysis it proves, exceptionally, to have no content whatever. It would be surprising if the first limb of one and the same subsection were intended to be specific application of the general principle in the preceding subsection, and the second limb to be a radical departure from it. If Parliament had intended to introduce a new rule of the nature contended for, their Lordships would have expected this to be done by clearer and more specific langugage than appears in the second limb of subsection (3).

Atkin L.J., in the course of that part of his judgment in *Millet* v. *Van Heek & Co.* [1921] 2 K.B. 369 which dealt with the question whether the second limb of section 51(3) applied to cases of anticipatory breach, expressed the view, at p. 377, that it was anomalous that a plaintiff should not only have the option, but be compelled, to fix his damages in reference to the time when the repudiation takes place. It appears to their Lordships that a plaintiff in such a case is not necessarily so compelled. He is not required to accept the repudiation, and if he does not do so the repudiation has no effect. He may wait until there has been an actual failure by the defendant to perform the contract, either on account of an unmet demand or on account of a reasonable time having elapsed without delivery. In this event the damages would be assessed, not at the date of the unaccepted repudiation, but at the date of the actual failure to perform. A more important consideration, in their Lordships' view, is that if the plaintiff did accept the repudiation, and if the market were to fall substantially up to the time when in the event the contract ought to have been performed, the plaintiff would be placed in a better position than if there had been due performance. This would represent an important inroad on a fundamental principle of assessment of damages, namely, that they should be no more than compensatory. In the result, their Lordships have not been satisfied that *Millett* v. *Van Heek & Co.* was wrongly decided, and considering that the decision has stood for 57 years without being subjected to any published criticism, and has no doubt been acted on in many cases, they are of opinion that it ought to be applied in the present case. Their Lordships therefore affirm the principle that the second limb of section 51(3) of the Act of 1893 and of section 53(3) of the Hong Kong Ordinance, does not apply in any case of anticipatory breach of contract.

It follows that the majority of the Full Court in the present case were wrong to assess damages on the basis of the market price of cotton yarn on July 31, 1973. The applicable rule for ascertaining the measure of damages is that contained in section 53(2) of the Hong Kong Ordinance, namely that it is 'the estimated loss directly and naturally resulting, in the ordinary course of events, from the seller's breach of contract.' As their Lordships have noticed, the contract here was for delivery of the cotton yarn in such instalments as might be demanded by the buyers upon reasonable notice. It was common ground between the parties that the period of reasonable notice for delivery of the balance of 424.20 bales of yarn was one month. Some suggestion was made that, when the buyers by their letter dated July 21, 1973 'earnestly requested' the sellers to deliver four bales a day from July 26 onwards, this constituted a demand for delivery in terms of the contract. But upon a consideration of the whole terms of the letter their Lordships are of opinion that it cannot be so construed. The buyers did not accept the seller's repudiation of July 31, and at any time thereafter could have demanded delivery of the balance of yarn on one month's notice. That situation continued until November 28, 1973, when the buyers issued and served their writ, thereby accepting the repudiation and rescinding the contract. November 28 was thus the last day upon which the buyer could have given reasonable notice requiring delivery of the yarn, and in their Lordships' opinion the appropriate date upon which to consider the market price of yarn for the purpose of assessing damages was one month thereafter, namely December 28, 1973.

Notes

1. S. 53 of the Hong Kong Sale of Goods Ordinance may be taken to be the same as s. 51 of the Sale of Goods Act.
2. The reader may be puzzled as to why the court needed to treat the whole of the yarn as not delivered on one particular date, whereas there had in fact been a series of non-deliveries. The answer is that the pleadings had alleged only one breach, and leave to amend to plead the earlier breaches separately had been refused.

If the 'innocent' party accepts the repudiation, the contract is at an end, and the right to damages arises. Consequently, he comes under the normal duty to mitigate his loss. For a buyer on a rising market this means he should take steps to cover by buying in substitute goods. If he fails to do this, he may have his damages limited to the amount for which he could have covered.[77] If, on the other hand, he accepts the repudiation and the market falls up to the time when the contract ought to have been performed, he is limited to damages fixed by reference to the contract/market difference at that date.[78] *Mutatis mutandae*, the same presumably applies to sellers: if the market is falling, they should dispose of the goods after accepting the repudiation, but if it is rising, presumably their damages will be fixed at the date for acceptance.

A further problem with anticipatory repudiation is that there is no requirement in the Act that the innocent party should exercise his election to accept the repudiation in a commercially reasonable manner. Outside the Act there is only dicta of Lord Reid in *White & Carter Councils* v. *McGregor*[79] to suggest that the right to elect may not be absolutely unfettered; indeed the actual decision in that case is authority for the view that the innocent party can elect as he pleases – a view which is likely to lead to economically wasteful results. In the absence of any suitable English authority, consider the following hypothetical case.

A agrees in January to manufacture a machine for B, delivery to take place on 1 October. In July, when the machine is half completed, B repudiates. Let us assume that the value of the half-completed machine is £2,000 as scrap. The machine when completed was to cost the buyer £60,000, of which the seller's profit was £15,000.

Let us say that the seller's loss in July is the cost of labour and materials to date, say £20,000, less the £2,000 = £18,000. Whether or not he should be entitled in addition to the full £15,000 profit, will depend on whether or not he is a lost-volume seller (p. 130, below). If he is not, i.e. if his order-book is overflowing, his loss is only a part of that profit. Furthermore, by stopping production, he may be able to save on fixed overheads by shutting down that particular part of his factory[80] (this could apply even if his order-book overflowed). By continuing to make the machine, the seller increases the buyer's loss, and produces an economically inefficient result – he has tied up valuable production capacity in an unwanted machine.

If you consider that in the above case, the seller should be under a duty to stop production, would you take into account the fact that a seller in doing so might have to lay off labour (which might include scarce skilled labour) and be liable to make redundancy payments?

(b) Actual breach

(i) *Instalment contracts*

It was pointed out at the beginning of this section that the parties may attempt to seize on trivial breaches as a way of escaping from a bad bargain. Instalment contracts, which by their nature extend over a period of time may be particularly susceptible to this. Where goods are to be delivered by instalments, and the seller fails to deliver one or more instalment, or the buyer fails to pay for it, is such breach by either party a repudiation of the whole contract?

MAPLE FLOCK CO. v. UNIVERSAL FURNITURE PRODUCTS (WEMBLEY) LIMITED [1934] 1 K.B. 148 (C.A.)

The plaintiffs contracted to sell 100 tons of rag flock to the defendants, delivery by instalments of 1½ tons per week, each to be separately paid for. The sixteenth instalment was defective, and the defendant purported to treat the whole contract as repudiated by the plaintiffs.

LORD HOWARD C.J. delivered the judgement of the court:
With the help of these authorities we deduce that the main tests to be considered in applying the sub-section to the present case are, first, the ratio quantitatively which the breach bears to the contract as a whole, and secondly the degree of probability or improbability that such a breach will be repeated. On the first point, the delivery complained of amounts to no more than 1½ tons out of a contract for 100 tons. On the second point, our conclusion is that the chance of the breach being repeated is practically negligible. We assume that the sample found defective fairly represents the bulk; but bearing in mind the judge's finding that the breach was extraordinary and that the appellant's business was carefully conducted, bearing in mind also that the appellants were warned, and bearing in mind that the delivery complained of was an isolated instance out of 20 satisfactory deliveries actually made both before and after the instalment objected to, we hold that it cannot reasonably be inferred that similar breaches would occur in regard to subsequent deliveries. Indeed, we do not understand that the learned Judge came to any different conclusion. He seems, however, to have decided against the appellants on a third and separate ground, that is, that a delivery not satisfying the Government requirements would or might lead to the respondents being prosecuted under the Act. Though we think he exaggerates the likelihood of the respondents in such a case being held responsible, we do not wish to underrate the gravity to the respondents of their being even prosecuted. But

we cannot follow the Judge's reasoning that the bare possibility, however remote, of this happening would justify the respondents in rescinding in this case. There may indeed be such cases, as also cases where the consequences of a single breach of contract may be so serious as to involve a frustration of the contract and justify rescission, or furthermore, the contract might contain an express condition that a breach would justify rescission, in which case effect would be given to such a condition by the Court. But none of these circumstances can be predicated of this case. We think the deciding factor here is the extreme improbability of the breach being repeated, and on that ground, and on the isolated and limited character of the breach complained of, there was, in our judgment, no sufficient justification to entitle the respondents to refuse further deliveries as they did.

The appeal must accordingly be allowed and judgment entered for the appellants, with costs here and below, for damages for their breach of contract in refusing further deliveries.

Note

The effect of holding that the contract is an instalment contract and applying the Maple Flock test is to reduce the possibility of the 'innocent' party using a slight breach as an excuse for sliding out of a bad bargain. Why then do we define instalment contract so narrowly – i.e. require instalments to be separately *paid for*? Compare Uniform Commercial Code (1978 text) 2-612(1) which defines it as 'the delivery of goods in separate lots, to be separately accepted'.

For a good example of a seller trying to use non-payment to slide out of a contract see *Plotnick* v. *Pennsylvania Smelting*.[81]

(ii) *Other contracts*

By the nature of things, the scope for sellers to slide out of disadvantageous contracts is more limited than that of buyers, and it is in any event provided by s. 10 that stipulations as to time of payment are not deemed to be of the essence. The problem is more likely to arise the other way round, where buyers may seize on a trifling defect in the goods. It is to be noted in the first place that a defective tender by the seller is not necessarily a repudiation of itself. As Lord Devlin wrote:[82] 'A tender of . . . goods under a contract for the sale of goods in a condition that does not comply with the terms of the contract, is not a breach. What creates the breach in such a case is the failure to tender within the contract time [goods] in a condition that does comply with the contract.'[83] Nevertheless, in many areas the seller will have no second chance to substitute a conforming delivery. In such a case if the market has fallen below the contract price, the buyer's right to reject is an extremely valuable one. The defect seized upon might be quite trivial, and the Act contains no provision allowing the seller an opportunity to 'cure' equivalent to 2-508(2) U.C.C. The following case provides a very good illustration of this problem.

CEHAVE v. BREMER HANDELGESELLSCHAFT [1976] 1 Q.B. 44

The appellants agreed to sell to the respondents 12,000 metric tons of US citrus pulp pellets for use in cattle food. There were two contracts for 6,000 tons each, to be delivered by 1,000-ton instalments c.i.f. Rotterdam. The contracts included the term 'shipment to be made in good condition'. Three or four were satisfactorily delivered. The shipment out of which the dispute arose was made in May 1971. The ship took on about 3,400 tons of pellets in Florida, the price was paid on 14 May 1971 and the shipping documents handed over. By 21 May, when the ship arrived in Rotterdam, the market price had fallen considerably. The buyer rejected on the ground that the goods were not in good condition: about a third of the cargo, the contents of one hold, were slightly damaged.

Thereafter followed what the Master of the Rolls called 'an atonishing sequence of events'. The cargo had been discharged into lighters in Rotterdam, and on 1 June the lighter-owners, represented by the same lawyers as the buyers, applied for and obtained in the Rotterdam County Court an order of sale. The sellers were not informed of the application. The cargo was bought by an importer, who resold it to the buyers at the same price and on the same terms as he had acquired it. That price was less than a third of the contract price. The buyers thereupon used the pulp to manufacture cattle food as originally had been intended. Moreover, the arbitration tribunal found as a fair inference from the evidence that the importer had acted on behalf of the buyers.

The arbitration tribunal (the Board of the Grain and Food Trade Association) in its special case stated, found that, on the balance of probability, not all the goods in No. 1 hold were shipped in good condition, and also that, although the pellets were 'merchantable' in a commercial sense, there was a breach of section 14(2) [the old merchantable quality section] of the Sale of Goods Act, and that the buyers might therefore reject the whole cargo. Mocatta J. affirmed this finding. (See [1974] 2 W. Rep. 216.) In doing so he rejected an argument put forward by counsel for the sellers, relying on *Hong Kong Fir Shipping* v. *Kawasaki*, [1962] 2 Q.B. 26 that in view of the fact that the pellets had been used for the purpose for which they had been bought, there was no breach justifying rejection. He held that the Sale of Goods Act dichotomy, conditions/warranties, was exclusive. The consequences of so holding was that the buyers acquired for about £30,000 goods they had contracted to buy for £100,000. The Court of Appeal, however, in a unanimous decision, allowed the sellers' appeal holding *inter alia* that the express term was an intermediate stipulation which gave no right to reject unless the breach went to the root of the contract, and that the goods were 'merchantable' within the meaning of section 14(2).

LORD DENNING M.R.

The general law apart from the sale of goods

For the last 300 or 400 years the courts have had to grapple with this problem: in what circumstances can a party, who is in breach himself of a stipulation of the contract, call upon the other side to perform his part or sue him for non-performance? At one time the solution was thought to depend on the nature of the stipulation itself, and not on the extent of the breach or its consequences. Under the old forms of pleading, a plaintiff had to aver and prove that he had performed all conditions precedent or that he was ready and willing to perform them. The question, therefore, was whether the stipulation (which he had broken) was a condition precedent or not: or, in the terminology of the 18th century, whether it was an *independent* covenant (the breach of which did not debar him from suing the other side), or a *dependent* on the plaintiff performing his). The distinction was well stated by Serjeant Williams in his notes to *Pordage* v. *Cole* (1669) 1 Wms. Saund. 319, 320b:

> '. . . where there are several covenants, promises or agreements, which are *independent* of each other, one party may bring an action against the other for a breach of his covenants, etc. without averring a performance of the covenants, etc. on his the plaintiff's part; and it is no excuse for the defendant to allege in his plea a breach of the covenants, etc. on the part of the plaintiff; . . . But where the covenants, etc. are *dependent*, it is necessary for the plaintiff to aver and prove a performance of the covenants, etc. on his part, to entitle himself to an action for the breach of the covenants on the part of the defendant; . . .'

Although that division was treated as exhaustive, nevertheless, when the courts came to apply it, they had regard to the extent of the breach. This was done by Lord Mansfield in 1777 in the great case of *Boone* v. *Eyre* (1779) 1 Hy.Bl. 273n., of which there was no satisfactory record until Lord Kenyon in 1796 produced a manuscript note of it: see *Campbell* v. *Jones* (1796) 6 Term.Rep. 570, 573 and *Glazbrook* v. *Woodrow* (1799) 8 Term.Rep. 366, 373. It is summarised in the notes to *Cutter* v. *Powell* (1795) 6 Term.Rep. 320 (*Smith's Leading Cases*, 13th ed. (1929), vol 2, pp. 16-17). The plaintiff conveyed to the defendant a plantation in the West Indies, together with the stock of negroes on it, in consideration of £500 down and an annuity of £100 a year, and covenanted that he had a good title to the plantation and was lawfully possessed of the negroes. Some time later the defendant discovered that the plaintiff had no title to the negroes and stopped paying the annuity. The court held that the defendant was liable to pay the annuity. He could not escape simply because the plaintiff had not 'a title to a few negroes'. His remedy was to bring a cross-action for damages. It would be different 'if the plaintiff had no title at all to the plantation itself' (see 8 Term.Rep. 366, 374: for then the plaintiff could not have recovered the annuity). In the language of those times, if the breach went to the whole consideration, the covenant was considered to be a condition precedent and the defendant could plead the breach in bar of the action: but if the breach went

> 'only to a part, where a breach may be paid for in damages, there the defendant has a remedy on his covenant, and shall not plead it as a condition precedent' (1 Hy.Bl. 273n.).

In short, if the breach went to the root of the matter, the stipulation was to be considered a condition precedent: but if the breach did not go to the root, the stipulation was considered to be an independent covenant which could be compensated for in damages: see *Davidson* v. *Gwynne* (1810) 12 East 381, 389, *per* Lord Ellenborough C.J.; *Ellen* v. *Topp* (1851) 7 Exch. 424, 441; and *Graves* v. *Legg* (1854) 9 Exch. 709, 716.

Apart from those cases of 'breach going to the root,' the courts at the same time were developing the doctrine of 'anticipatory breach'. When one party, before the day when he is obliged to perform his part, declares in advance that he will not perform it when the day comes or by his conduct evinces an intention not to perform it, the other may elect to treat his declaration or conduct as a breach going to the root of the matter and to treat himself as discharged from further performance: see *Hochster* v. *De La Tour* (1853) 2 E. & B. 678. By his prior declaration or conduct, the guilty party is said to repudiate the contract. The word 'repudiation' should be confined to those cases of an *anticipatory* breach, but it is also used in connection with cases of an *actual* breach going to the root of the contract: see *Heyman* v. *Darwins Ltd* [1942] A.C. 356, 378-379 by Lord Wright. All of them were gathered together by Lord Blackburn in his famous speech in *Mersey Steel and Iron Co.* v. *Naylor, Benzon & Co.* (1884) 9 App.Cas. 434, 443-444:

> 'The rule of law, as I always understood it, is that where there is a contract in which there are two parties, each side having to do something (it is so laid down in the notes to *Pordage* v. *Cole*, 1 Wms. Saund. 319, 320) if you see that the failure to perform one part of it goes to the root of the contract, goes to the foundation of the whole, it is a good defence to say, "I am not going on to perform my part of it when that which is the root of the whole and the substantial consideration for my performance is defeated by your misconduct." . . . I repeatedly asked Mr Cohen whether or not he could find any authority which justified him in saying that every breach of a contract . . . must be considered to go to the root of the contract, and he produced no such authority. There are many cases in which the breach may do so; it depends upon the con-

struction of the contract.'

Those last words are clearly a reference to a 'condition' strictly so called, in which any breach entitled the other to be discharged from further performance. But the earlier words are quite general. They refer to all terms other than conditions strictly so called.

The Sale of Goods Act
Such was the state of the law when the Sale of Goods Act 1893 was passed on February 20, 1894. I have studied the then current edition of *Benjamin, Sale of Personal Property*, 4th ed. (1888), and the little books which Judge Chalmers wrote before (1890) and after the Act (*Chalmers' Sale of Goods Act*, 1893, 1st ed. (1894), and the proceedings in Parliament. These show that until the year 1893 there was much confusion in the use of the words 'condition' and 'warranty'. But that confusion was removed by the Act itself and by the judgment of Bowen L.J. in *Bentsen* v. *Taylor, Sons & Co.* [1893] 2 Q.B. 274, 280. Thenceforward those words were used by lawyers as terms of art. The difference between them was that if the promisor broke a *condition* in any respect, however slight, it gave the other party a right to be quit of his obligations and to sue for damages: unless he by his conduct waived the condition, in which case he was bound to perform his future obligations but could sue for the damage he had suffered. If the promisor broke a *warranty* in any respect, however serious, the other party was not quit of his future obligations. He had to perform them. His only remedy was to sue for damages: see *The Mihalis Angelos* [1971] 1 Q.B. 164, 193 and *Wickman Machine Tool Sales Ltd* v. *L. Schuler A.G.* [1972] 1 W.L.R. 840, 851.

Now that division was not exhaustive. It left out of account the vast majority of stipulations which were neither 'conditions' nor 'warranties' strictly so called: but were intermediate stipulations, the effect of which depended on the breach. The cases about these stipulations were legion. They stretched continuously from *Boone* v. *Eyre*, 1 Hy.Bl. 273n., in 1777 to *Mersey Steel and Iron Co. Ltd* v. *Naylor, Benzon & Co.* (1884) 9 App.Cas. 434. I cannot believe that Parliament in 1893 intended to give the go-by to all these cases: or to say that they did not apply to the sale of goods. Those cases expressed the rules of the common law. They were preserved by section 61(2) of the Act of 1893, which said:

> 'The rules of the common law, including the law merchant, save in so far as they are inconsistent with the express provisions of this Act . . .shall continue to apply to contracts for the sale of goods.'

There was nothing in the Act inconsistent with those cases. So they continued to apply.

In 1962 in the *Hong Kong Fir Shipping Co. Ltd* v. *Kawasaki Kisen Kaisha Ltd* [1962] 2 Q.B. 26, the Court of Appeal drew the attention to this vast body of case law. They showed that, besides conditions and warranties, strictly so called, there are many stipulations of which the effect depends on this: if the breach goes to the root of the contract, the other party is entitled to treat himself as discharged: but if it does not go to the root, he is not. In my opinion, the principle embodied in these cases applies to contracts for the sale of goods just as to all other contracts.

The task of the court can be stated simply in the way in which Upjohn L.J. stated it at p. 64. First, see whether the stipulation, on its true construction, is a condition strictly so called, that is, a stipulation such that, for any breach of it, the other party is entitled to treat himself as discharged. Second, if it is not such a condition, then look to the extent of the actual breach which has taken place. If it is such as to go to the root of the contract, the other party is entitled to treat himself as discharged: but, otherwise, not. To this may be added an anticipatory breach. If the one party, before the day on which he is due to perform his part, shows by his words or conduct that he will not perform it in a vital respect when the day comes, the other party is entitled to treat himself as discharged.

'Shipped in good condition'

This brings me back to the particular stipulation in this case: 'Shipped in good condition.' Was this a condition strictly so called, so that *any* breach of it entitled the buyer to reject the goods? Or was it an intermediate stipulation, so that the buyer cannot reject unless the breach is so serious as to go to the root of the contract?

If there was any previous authority holding it to be a *condition* strictly so called, we should abide by it, just as we did with the clause 'expected ready to load': see *Finnish Government (Ministry of Food)* v. *H. Ford & Co. Ltd* (1921) 6 Ll.L.Rep. 188; *The Mihalis Angelos* [1971] 1 Q.B. 164. But, there is no such authority with the clause 'shipped in good condition'. I regard this clause as comparable to a clause as to quality, such as 'fair average quality.' If a small portion of the goods sold was a little below that standard, it would be met by commercial men by an allowance off the price. The buyer would have no right to reject the whole lot unless the divergence was serious and substantial: see *Biggin & Co. Ltd* v. *Permanite Ltd* [1951] 1 K.B. 422, 439, *per* Devlin J. and *Christopher Hill Ltd* v. *Ashington Piggeries Ltd* (1972) A.C. 441, 511, *per* Lord Diplock. That is shown in this very case by clause 5 in form no. 100 which contains percentages of contamination, below which there is a price allowance, and above which there is a right in the buyer to reject. Likewise with the clause 'shipped in good condition.' If a small portion of the whole cargo was not in good condition and arrived a little unsound, it should be met by a price allowance. The buyers should not have a right to reject the whole cargo unless it was serious and substantial. This is borne out by the difficulty which often arises (as in this case) on a c.i.f. contract as to whether the damage was done before shipment or took place after shipment: for in the latter case the buyer would have no claim against the seller but would be left to his claim against the insurers. So, as matter of good sense, the buyer should be bound to accept the goods and not reject them unless there is a serious and substantial breach, fairly attributable to the seller.

In my opinion, therefore, the term 'shipped in good condition' was not a condition strictly so called: nor was it a warranty strictly so called. It was one of those intermediate stipulations which gives no right to reject unless the breach goes to the root of the contract.

On the facts stated by the board of appeal, I do not think the buyer was entitled to reject these instalments of the contract. The board only said that 'not all the goods in hold no. 1 were shipped in good condition.' That does not say how many were bad. In any case, their condition cannot have been very bad, seeing that all of them were in fact used for the intended purpose. The breach did not go to the root of the contract. The buyer is entitled to damages, but not to rejection.

Merchantable

The Board of Appeal made this finding:

> 'The goods in hold 1 were "merchantable" on arrival at Rotterdam in a commercial sense, though at a lower price than would be paid for sound goods; we find and hold, however, that they were not "of merchantable quality" within the meaning of the phrase when used in the Sale of Goods Act 1893.'

The board of appeal were not lawyers: but they had a legal adviser. And I am afraid that in reaching that finding they were not advised correctly. The statute uses the words 'merchantable quality' in a commercial sense. The board should, therefore, have applied it in the commercial sense. They should not have been persuaded to give it some other 'statutory sense.'

Now we were taken through many of the definitions which have been given by judges of 'merchantable quality,' particularly that of Dixon J. in *Australian Knitting Mills Ltd* v. *Grant* (1933) 50 C.L.R. 387, 418; of Lord Wright in *Cammell Laird & Co. Ltd* v. *Manganese, Bronze & Brass Co. Ltd* [1934] A.C. 402, 430, as amended by Lord Reid in *Hardwick Game Farm* v. *Suffolk Agricultural Poultry Producers Association* [1969] 2 A.C. 31, 77 and by Lord Guest in *B.S. Brown & Son Ltd* v. *Craiks Ltd* [1970] 1 W.L.R. 752, 758. But, as Lord Reid pointed out in that case, at p. 754:

> '. . . judicial observations can never be regarded as complete definitions: they must be read in light of the facts and issues raised in the particular case. I do not think it is possible to frame, except in the vaguest terms, a definition of "merchantable quality" which can apply to every kind of case.'

For myself, I think the definition in the latest statute is the best that has yet been devised. It is contained in section 7(2) of the Supply of Goods (Implied Terms) Act 1973. The statute itself only applies to contracts made after May 18, 1973. But the definition seems to me appropriate for contracts made before it. It runs as follows:

> 'Goods of any kind are of merchantable quality within the meaning of this Act if they are as fit for the purpose or purposes for which goods of that kind are commonly bought as it is reasonable to expect having regard to any description applied to them, the price (if relevant) and all other relevant circumstances; and any reference in this Act to unmerchantable goods shall be construed accordingly.'

In applying that definition, it is as well to remember that, by the statute, we are dealing with an implied *condition*, strictly so called, and not a warranty. For any breach of it, therefore, the buyer is entitled to *reject* the goods: or, alternatively, if he chooses to accept them or has accepted them, he has a remedy in damages. In these circumstances, I should have thought a fair way of testing merchantability would be to ask a commercial man: was the breach such that the buyer should be able to reject the goods? In answering that question the commercial man would have regard to the various matters mentioned in the new statutory definition. He would, of course, have regard to the purpose for which goods of that kind are commonly bought. If a buyer buys 'waste silk' and it is of no use for the purpose of 'waste silk,' he can reject it: see *Gardiner* v. *Gray* (1815) 4 Camp. 144. If he buys dates for food and they are of no use for food, he can reject them: see *Asfar & Co.* v. *Blundell* [1896] 1 Q.B. 123, 127. But if he buys groundnuts for cattlefood, and they can reasonably be used for cattlefood, he may not be able to reject them, even though they are not suitable for poultry; see *Hardwick Game Farm* v. *Suffolk Agricultural Poultry Producers Association* [1969] 2 A.C. 31. The commercial man would also, of course, have regard to the description applied to them. If motor horns are sold, expressly or impliedly, as 'new' and then the buyer finds that they are dented and scratched, he ought to be able to reject them: see *Jackson* v. *Rotax Motor & Cycle Co.* [1910] 2 K.B. 937. If they are sold as 'secondhand' or 'shop soiled,' then he must take them as they are: see *Bartlett* v. *Sidney Marcus Ltd* [1965] 1 W.L.R. 1013; unless there is something radically wrong with them. He would also have regard to the price. If they are sold at the market price, the buyer would expect them to be of good quality and condition; and, if they were not, he would be able to reject them: see *Jones* v. *Just* (1868) L.R. 3 Q.B. 197 (much better reported in 9 B. & S. 141); and *B.S. Brown & Son Ltd* v. *Craiks Ltd* [1970] 1 W.L.R. 752, 754-755, *per* Lord Reid: but, if they are sold at a 'cut' price or 'bargain' price, or a lower price, he would have to put up with something less. He would not be entitled to reject them simply because they were not perfect. The commercial man would also have regard to any other relevant circumstances. If there was a clause, express or implied, which would give the buyer an allowance off the price for the particular shortcomings, such that a commercial man would say: 'The buyer is entitled to a price allowance but not to reject them' – again the goods would be of merchantable quality. The buyer would be entitled to an allowance or damages in lieu, but not entitled to reject the lot.

Our present case comes within that last illustration. These citrus pulp pellets were bought for cattle food. That was the purpose for which such pellets are commonly bought. They were as fit for that purpose as it was reasonable to expect. That is shown by the fact that they were actually used for that purpose. Some of them arrived damaged, but not to such an extent that the buyer was entitled to reject the cargo in both holds, or either of them. That damage was such as to entitle the buyer to an allowance off the price for breach of the clause 'shipped in good condition': but not such as to entitle him to reject the lot on the ground that it was not of 'merchantable quality.' That is, I think, what the board of appeal meant when they found that the goods were 'merchantable' on arrival at Rotterdam in a commercial sense, though at a lower price than would be paid for sound goods. In short, the buyers are entitled to an allowance or damages for the damaged goods, but not entitled to reject the lot. This makes commercial good sense. It often happens that the market price falls between the making of the contract and the time for delivery. In such a situation, it is not that a buyer should be allowed to reject a whole consignment of goods just because a small quantity are not up to the contract quality or condition. The proper remedy is a price allowance and not complete rejection. I feel sure that is what the board of appeal thought in this case. They only found otherwise because they thought the law constrained them to do so. Their instinct was right. Having found that in a commercial sense the goods were merchantable, there was no breach of section 14(2).

Damages

In my opinion, therefore, the buyers were not entitled to reject the goods. They are, however, entitled to damages for the difference in value between the damaged goods and sound goods on arrival at Rotterdam. The case must be remitted to the board for this to be determined.

I would allow the appeal, accordingly.

Questions

1. To what extent is the difference between Mocatta J. and the Court of Appeal in this case the difference between 'objectivist' and 'subjectivist' approaches? See pp. 53 et seq. above.
2. Would the goods have been merchantable within the definition contained in s. 14(6)?
3. Refer back to the decision of *Arcos* v. *Ronaasen* (p. 59) and *re Moore* v. *Landauer* (p. 59). To what extent might the outcome in those cases differ were they to come before the courts today?

(2) BUYER'S AND SELLER'S ACTIONS FOR DAMAGES

(a) Buyer's damages for non-delivery

S. 51, which deals with the buyer's remedy of damages for non-delivery, mirrors s. 50 which deals with damages for non-acceptance. As with s. 50(2), the '*Hadley* v. *Baxendale*' rule is set out (in s. 5(2)),[84] and thereafter follows the *prima facie* rule that where there is an available market for the goods the measure of damages is ascertained by the difference between the contract price and the market price at the time or times when the goods ought to have been delivered, or if no time was fixed, then at the time of refusal to deliver (s. 51(3)). It must be pointed out that s. 51(3) is not the same thing as the Hadley principle:[85] the plaintiff may recover more or less under it than his true loss. In pure commodity dealings, 'sales in a string' by chains of dealers, it may be pure chance whether goods exist to cover the sales. If dealers expect the market to rise they buy more than they sell; if they expect it to fall, they sell more than they buy. Consequently any particular sale may not be covered by any particular purchase of goods. In these circumstances, the artificial rule of s. 51(3) is a good one.[86] Where by contrast the buyer actually wants possession of goods, s. 51(3) is unlikely to give him his true damages. If the market falls between the time of delivery and the time he 'covers', having learnt of the non-delivery by buying elsewhere, s. 51(3) will overcompensate him. If by contrast the market rises, it will undercompensate him. The Uniform Commercial Code (1978 text) sensibly provides that in this latter case the buyer may recover the difference between the cost of cover and the contract price (2-712).

S. 51 applies not only to a failure to deliver any goods at all: in principle it should apply where non-conforming goods are supplied and the buyer rejects. The judge in the following case seems to have assumed that such a defective delivery amounted to a non-delivery.

MILLARS MACHINERY CO. v. DAVID WAY (1934) Com. Cas. 204

BRANSON J.

This action is brought by the plaintiffs, a firm of engineers, makers of gravel-washing plant, to recover the balance of the contract price of a 20-ton gravel-washer, with various accessories. The defendants have paid £350 on account, and the plaintiffs sue for the balance. The defendants, who own gravel pits, were minded in January, 1933, to open up a new pit and instal a gravel-washing plant in order to supply gravel to road-making authorities or other people who wanted washed and graded gravel. The machinery was delivered to the defendants' gravel pit in March, 1933. It was erected by the plaintiffs and various attempts were made to demonstrate that it would do the work which the contract provided that it should do. It did not do the work, and the plaintiffs from time to time made alterations in it in order to make it do the work. Finally, on June 12, 1933, the defendants purported to reject the machine as not being in accordance with the contract, and they counterclaim for the money which they have already paid in part payment of the contract price and for damages for the plaintiffs' breach of contract.

What are the damages here? I think, as I have said that there is no answer to the claim for the return of the £350. Then the defendants say that they have had to replace this machine by another which has cost more than the price agreed to be paid to the plaintiffs for their machine. They also claim for the cost of labour supplied for the erection of the plaintiffs' machine and for the cost of washed gravel which the defendants had to purchase to fulfil a contract with the Bucks County Council. Normally speaking, if a person contracts to deliver goods to another and fails to do so the damages are the difference between the price of the goods which he ought to have delivered and the market price. Here the plaintiffs agreed to supply a machine which would do certain work; they broke their contract, and if the defendants could have gone into the market and bought another machine the damages would have been the difference between the price which they had agreed to pay the plaintiffs and the price of the other machine. The position is in fact more complicated because these machines are not standardized articles which can be bought anywhere; they have to be manufactured to meet the circumstances of the particular customer. One has to see what the defendants could reasonably have done to make good the damage occasioned to them by the plaintiffs' breach of contract. According to their evidence they did the only possible thing, they went to people who could supply one of these machines at short notice and had to pay some £1,450 for it. I think the proper measure of damages is the sum which the defendants had to spend to put themselves in the position in which they would have been if the plaintiffs had carried out their contract. Approaching the matter from the point of view of a jury I think it a fair estimate to say that the defendants were out of pocket to the extent of £426 in respect of machinery. If the defendants get that, and the £350 which they have paid, they will be as nearly as I can estimate in the position in which they would have been had there been no breach of the plaintiffs' contract. If they had got a good machine from the plaintiffs they would have had to bear the cost of labour for which they counterclaim, and if they get the difference in value of the plant they cannot fairly charge those expenses over again.

Question

The judge did not in fact refer to the Act, but do you think his decision amounts in effect to an application of s. 51(2) or s. 51(3)?

Note

The result in *Millars* v. *Way* seems to be correct. The curious view has been expressed, however, that in such a situation the plaintiff should recover only the deposit paid (£350), and not the consequential loss. This *inter alia* was argued in the following case.

MASON v. BURNINGHAM [1949] 2 K.B. 545

The plaintiff bought a typewriter from the defendant for £20 and subsequently spent £11 10s on overhauling it. The typewriter had been stolen and she had to return it to the true owner. She claimed against the defendant for breach of the warranty of quiet possession implied by s. 12. The issue dealt with here was whether she was entitled merely to a return of her money, or the £11 10s in addition.

SINGLETON L.J.
The particulars of claim in this action, claim under both heads of s. 12, but in this court Mr Leon has put forward only that there was breach of an implied warranty that the buyer should have and enjoy quiet possession of the goods. Mr O'Sullivan in his submission to the court submitted that there was and was alleged to be a breach of the implied condition in sub-s. 1, on the part of the seller that he had a right to sell the goods, and Mr O'Sullivan submitted that that would give rise only to a claim for the return of the money paid and that it would not give a general right of action for damages. It appears to me that that matter has really little to do with this case, because in any event, if there was breach of the implied condition, the plaintiff was entitled to treat that as a breach of warranty.

As regards the damages, Mr O'Sullivan submitted that it was not shown that the defendant had any foreknowledge that this kind of damage might flow in case there was a breach. He further submitted that there was no evidence to show that the overhaul of the typewriter took place at once or soon after the purchase, and, unless that was shown, he submitted the damage would not flow and did not flow naturally from the breach. No such point as the second of those points was raised at the hearing at the court below, and no suggestion whatever was made to the plaintiff that she did not send the typewriter to be overhauled soon after she purchased it. It was accepted, as far as one can see, that she had in fact done so.

On the submission that the defendant had no foreknowledge that this kind of damage might flow, we were referred to the judgment of this court, delivered by Asquith L.J. in *Victoria Laundry (Windsor) Ltd* v. *Newman Industries Ltd* (1) [1949] 2 K.B. 528, and in particular to a passage in the judgment where the Lord Justice said: 'What was at that time reasonably foreseeable[87] depends on the knowledge then possessed by the parties, or, at all events, by the party who later commits the breach. For this purpose, knowledge "possessed" is of two kinds – one imputed, the other actual. Everyone, as a reasonable person, is taken to know the "ordinary course of things" and consequently what loss is liable to result from a breach of contract in that ordinary course'.

In the present case the learned county court judge found that the plaintiff 'behaved in a commonsense way,' that she did 'the ordinary and natural thing,' that what she did was 'quite naturally' done, and that it was 'right and proper'. In those circumstances I see no answer to this. That which followed followed directly and naturally: it resulted in 'the ordinary "course of events" ': damages have to be assessed under sub-s. 2 of s. 53 of the Sale of Goods Act, 1893, and those damages resulting from the breach of warranty on the part of the seller would have been if there had been no payment on account, the total amount of £20 which she paid for the typewriter and the amount she 'rightly' and 'properly' and 'naturally' expended to have it overhauled and put in proper order.

The learned county court judge in my view approached this matter from the wrong angle: he ought to have held that the plaintiff was entitled to the sum of £11 10s 0d, which was the balance remaining due, and in my view the judgment ought to be set aside and judgment entered for the plaintiff.

Note

The logic of the curious view that if the plaintiff had been confined to such remedy as she might have had on breach of condition, she might only have had *restitutio ad integrum*, ie. return of her £20, and not her consequential damages, is difficult to follow. It would appear to be clearly fallacious.[88] If that view were correct, the purchaser in *Millar* v. *Way* would presumably have been entitled only to a return of the price paid.

Displacement of the prima facie *rules*

Sub-sales

RE HALL & PIM'S ARBITRATION [1928] All E.R. Rep. 763

A specific cargo in a specific ship was sold to the buyers at 51s 9d a quarter. The buyers resold at 56s 9d a quarter. At the date for delivery the market price had fallen to 53s a quarter. The seller failed to deliver. Were the damages 56s 9d minus 51s 9d or 53s minus 51s 9d? *Held*: the appropriate measure was 56s 9d minus 51s 9d = 5s per quarter.

VISCOUNT HALDANE
I have come to the conclusion that the contract is one not merely for the sale of corn in bulk, but for the sale of the cargo of an individual ship which is either specifically identified or is to be so identified. This contract was effectively made on Nov. 3, 1925, and what took place

between the parties a little later neither adds anything to its binding character nor detracts from that character. I think further that the contract and the conditions which it incorporates show that it was contemplated that the cargo might be passed on by way of sub-sale if the buyer did not choose to keep it for himself, and tthat the seller in such a case contracted to put the buyer in a position to fulfil his sub-contracts if he entered into them. They were regarded by the terms of the original contract as sub-contracts which the original buyer was to be in a position to enter into, with stipulations which bound the original seller to enable the original buyer to fulfil them. Whether the latter was likely to enter into such sub-contracts and pass the cargo down a chain is not material. It is enough that the contract contemplated by its terms that he should have the right to do so if he chose. This being the case, there has been an admitted breach. The original seller has failed to deliver at the due date, and the buyer has been left open to claims from his sub-buyers based on the contracts made with them in reliance on the clauses in the document of Nov. 3.

In these circumstances I am of opinion that the measure of damages is clear. It is not merely the amount of damage, measured by loss in the market, which arises in the usual course of business from the breach. It extends whenever the special circumstances require this, to such possible damages as may reasonably be supposed to have been in the contemplation of both parties at the time they made the contract, as the probable result of the breach of it. This is in accordance with what is called the second branch of the rule in *Hadley* v. *Baxendale* (1954) 9 Ex. 341, a rule which is fully explained by LORD ESHER M.R. in *Hammond & Co.* v. *Bussey* (1887) 20 Q.B.D. 79. He points out that the principle is not to be confined to a sub-contract already actually made at the date of the original contract, but applies also to the case of a sub-contract which will probably be made. There is no doubt that the law is correctly explained in *Hammond & Co.* v. *Bussey* (1887) 20 Q.B.D. 79, and I am of opinion that the case before me depends on a question of construction which comes directly within it and must be answered in accordance with the buyer's contention.

Note

Atiyah points out[89] that had the sub-buyer sued the buyer, his damages would have been nil, because the market price was lower than the resale price, in response to Ogus's argument that the reason for the decision was that it was a sale and resale of a specific cargo, and the buyer could not have substituted other goods bought on the market at 53s in fulfilment of the resale. Is this an answer? What was the buyer's expectation interest in this case? Is this case a straightforward application of *Hadley* v. *Baxendale*?

The buyer's damages may also be limited by sub-sales, as the following case shows (it involved damages for late, rather than non-delivery).

WERTHEIM v CHICOUTINI PULP CO. [1911] A.C. 301 (P.C.)

The seller contracted to sell moist wood pulp to the buyer. At the date of delivery, the market price was 70s a ton, but at the time when the goods were in fact delivered, it was only 42s 6d a ton. The buyer, however, resold at 65s a ton. He claimed the difference between 70s and 42s 6d a ton, i.e. the difference between the market price of the pulp at the time when it ought to have been delivered and its price when it was delivered. It was held, however, that he was limited to the difference between 70s and his resale at 65s, that is, 5s.

LORD ATKINSON
The purchaser not having got his goods should receive by way of damages enough to enable him to buy similar goods in the open market. Similarly, when the delivery of goods purchased is delayed, the goods are presumed to have been at the time they should have been delivered worth to the purchaser what he could then sell them for, or buy others like them for, in the open market, and when they are in fact delivered they are similarly presumed to be for the same reason, worth to the purchaser what he could then sell for in that market, but if in fact the purchaser, when he obtains possession of the goods, sells them at a price greatly in advance of the then market value, that presumption is rebutted and the real value of the goods to him is proved by the very fact of this sale to be more than market value, and the loss he sustains must be measured by that price, unless he is, against all justice, to be permitted to make a profit by the breach of contract, be compensated for a loss he never suffered, and be put, as far as money can do it, not in the same position in which he would have been if the contract had been performed, but in a much better position.

Questions

1. The contract in this case did not contemplate a sub-sale. On what principle, then, were the plaintiff's damages limited?
2. Since the *prima facie* rule of s. 51(3) applies only to non-delivery, on what ground could the buyer in this case claim the contract/market difference at the date of delivery for a mere late delivery?

(b) Seller's damages for non-acceptance

S. 50(2) embodies the *Hadley* v. *Baxendale* principle[90] that the measure of damages is the estimated loss directly and naturally resulting, in the ordinary course of events, from the buyer's breach of contract. If the Act stopped here, all might be well. Unfortunately s. 50(3) goes on to provide that this measure is *prima facie* to be ascertained by the difference between the contract price and the market price and the market price at the time or times when the goods ought to have been accepted, or the time of refusal. In practice, sellers may well be unable to resell when the non-acceptance occurs. In the first place they may not *learn* of the non-acceptance for a day or so; secondly, it may be impractical to resell immediately. If, during this time, the market rises, the seller's resale will be at more than the contract price, and by claiming damages under s 50(3) he will therefore make an additional profit. If, on the other hand, the market falls still further, he will make a loss which is uncompensated. It is argued that since the seller cannot claim for this loss, it is only fair that he can retain any profit. A more satisfactory solution in either case would be, however, to give the seller his real loss and only his real loss.

Displacement of the prima facie *rule*

The problem of the lost-volume seller

(i) The seller has contracted to sell to the buyer *x* units of goods, the supply of which exceeds the demand. If the buyer repudiates, the seller has lost his profit on *x* number of units.
(ii) The seller has contracted to sell to the buyer *x* units of goods, the demand for which exceeds the supply. If the buyer repudiates, the seller's loss will be purely nominal, for he cannot sell more than those *x* number of units, and he can readily sell them elsewhere.

We would therefore wish to compensate the seller in case (i) but not in case (ii). But there is a problem: if these are goods with a fixed price, such as a new car, the damages under the contract/market differential of s. 50(3) are nil. The courts, however, have held the *prima facie* rule to be displaced in such a case: *Thompson* v. *Robinson (Gunmakers) Ltd.*[92] If, however, demand exceeds supply, the seller will recover only nominal damages.[93] The crucial problem for the seller is to prove loss of volume of sales. The following case explores this difficulty:

LAZENBY GARAGES v. WRIGHT [1976] 1 W.L.R. 459

The plaintiffs, dealers in second-hand cars, contracted to sell a BMW to the defendant for £1,670. The buyer subsequently repudiated, and the plaintiffs resold the car for £1,770. They claimed £345 damages from the defendant, the profit they would have made on that particular deal i.e. £1,670 less £1,325.

LORD DENNING M.R.
The cases show that if there are a number of new cars, all exactly of the same kind, available for sale, and the dealers can prove that they sold one car less than they otherwise would have done, they would be

entitled to damages amounting to their loss of profit on the one car: see the judgment of Upjohn J. in *W.L. Thompson Ltd* v. *Robinson (Gunmakers) Ltd* [1955] Ch. 177. The same has been held in the United States: *Torkomian* v. *Russell* (1916) 97 Atlantic Reporter 760 and *Stewart* v. *Hansen* (1923) 218 P.959; in Canada, *Mason & Risch Ltd* v. *Christner* (1920) 54 D.L.R. 653; and in Australia, *Cameron* v. *Campbell & Worthington Ltd* [1930] S.A.S.R. 402.

But it is entirely different in the case of a secondhand car. Each secondhand car is different from the next, even though it is the same make. The sales manager of the plaintiffs admitted in evidence that some secondhand cars, of the same make, even of the same year, may sell better than others of the same year. Some may sell quickly, others may be sluggish. You simply cannot tell why. But they are all different.

In the circumstances the cases about new cars do not apply. We have simply to apply to section 50 of the Sale of Goods Act 1893. There is no 'available market' for secondhand cars. So it is not subsection (3) but subsection (2). The measure of damages is the estimated loss resulting directly and naturally in the ordinary course of events from the buyer's breach of contract. That throws us back to the test of what could reasonably be expected to be in the contemplation of the parties as a natural consequence of the breach. The buyer in this case could not have contemplated that the dealer would sell one car less. At most he would contemplate that, if they resold this very car at a lower price, they would suffer by reason of that lower price and should recover the difference. But if they resold this very car at a higher price, they would suffer no loss.

Seeing that these plaintiffs resold this very car for £100 more than the sale to Mr Wright, they clearly suffered no damage at all. In my opinion the appeal should be allowed and judgment entered for the defendant.

Note

The combination of the problem of lost-volume sellers and the difficulties arising in relation to anticipatory repudiation give rise to some complex questions where the seller is a manufacturer of goods. See the example given at p. 113 above.

(c) Damages for breach of warranty

The buyer's remedy for breach of warranty is damages. These may be set off against the price or recovered by an action against the seller (s. 53(1)). The measure of these damages is the estimated loss directly and naturally resulting, in the ordinary course of events, from the breach of warranty (s. 53(2)). In the case of breach of warranty quality this is *prima facie* the difference between the value of the goods at the time of delivery to the buyer and the value they would have had if they had fulfilled the warranty (s. 53(3)). Arguably, s. 53(2) (like ss. 50(2) and 51(2)) enacts only the first 'limb' of *Hadley* v. *Baxendale*, and not the second 'limb', the 'reasonable contemplation' requirement, therefore. However, the Court of Appeal declined to interpret the section in this way in the following important case

H. PARSONS (LIVESTOCK) LTD v. UTTLEY INGHAM & CO. LTD [1978] 1 Q.B. 791

The defendants sold a hopper for storing pig nuts to the plaintiffs. Unfortunately, when the defendants installed it, they forgot to untape the ventilator. As a result, nuts stored in the hopper went mouldy, and pigs to which they had been fed developed *E. coli* (an intestinal infection) from which 254 died. The judge in the first instance held that the hopper as delivered was not reasonably fit for the purpose of storing pig nuts. He held that although he would not have been justified in finding either party would reasonably have contemplated that there was a serious possibility that feeding the pig nuts in a mouldy condition would cause the illness which occurred, because s. 53(2) enacted only the first 'limb' of the rule in *Hadley* v. *Baxendale* the defendants were liable for all the damages of which their breach was a cause (i.e. the second 'limb', the 'reasonable contemplation' requirement, was ousted by the statute).

SCARMAN L.J.

But it is necessary to note the essence – and the limits – of the findings [of the judge at first instance]. It is a finding that the parties could not reasonably be supposed to have had in contemplation that there was a serious possibility of mouldy nuts causing illness in the plaintiffs' pigs. It is not a finding that they could not reasonably have had in contemplation that a hopper unfit for its purpose of storing food in a condition suitable for feeding to the pigs might well lead to illness.

The judge's other findings of fact may be summarised as follows. He found that there was a warranty – its existence is not disputed by the defendants – to the effect that the hopper should be reasonably fit for the purpose of storing pignuts in a condition suitable for feeding to the plaintiffs' pigs. He found that the hopper, being unventilated, was not so fit; and this defect was a breach of the warranty, and that the pignuts were unfit by reason of the breach. He found that the plaintiffs' loss was caused by the breach of warranty. Upon the basis of these findings, the judge held that since the first question is whether 'the damage' claimed arises in the ordinary course of things from the breach, 'there is no need to have recourse to the question of the presumed contemplation.' He then considered the meaning of the implied term 'pleaded and admitted' that the hopper should be reasonably fit for the purpose of storing pignuts to be fed to the plaintiffs' pigs and reached the conclusion, which I respectfully think was inevitable, that it meant that, in so far as proper storage could achieve it, the hopper would keep the pignuts in a condition such as not to make the plaintiffs' pigs ill.

He stressed the importance to be attached to the particular nature of this herd of pigs – a very different set of animals from the ordinary farmyard pig – and to the intensive nature of the plaintiffs' farming operation, all of which matters were known to the defendants before contract. He stated his conclusion in these words:

> 'On this interpretation the inevitable conclusion from the findings I have already made would be that this hopper was not reasonably fit for that purpose and that this caused the nuts to become toxic and that the illness of the pigs was a direct and natural consequence of such breach and toxicity, and that the plaintiffs do not have to prove that the toxicity or its results were foreseeable to either party. To put it another way, once the question of foreseeability of the breach is eliminated, as it is by the absolute warranty, the consequences of the breach flow naturally from it.'

Mr Drake criticises strongly this part of the judgement. He says it is based on a misunderstanding of *Hadley* v. *Baxendale*, 9 Exch. 341 and he referred us to the well-known passage in Lord Reid's speech in *C. Czarnikow Ltd* v. *Koufos* [1967] 1 A.C. 350 where he said that it is not enough that in fact the plaintiff's loss was directly caused by the defendant's breach of contract. Lord Reid said, at p. 385:

> 'The crucial question is whether, on the information available to the defendant when the contract was made, he should, or the reasonable man in his position would, have realised that such loss was sufficiently likely to result from the breach of contract to make it proper to hold that the loss flowed naturally from the breach or that loss of that kind should have been within his contemplation.'

Notwithstanding his choice of language, I think the judge was making the approach which, according to Lord Reid, is the correct one. He was saying, in effect, that the parties to this contract must have appreciated that, if, as happened in the event, the hopper, unventilated, proved not to be suitable for the storage of pignuts to be fed to the plaintiff's pigs, it was not unlikely, there was a serious possibility, that the pigs would become ill. The judge put it this way:

> 'The *natural* result of feeding toxic food to animals is damage to their health and may be death, which is what occurred, albeit from a hitherto unknown disease and to particularly susceptible animals. There was therefore no need to invoke the question of *reasonable* contemplation in order to make the defendant liable' (my italicisation).

The judge in this critical passage is contrasting a natural result, i.e. one which people placed as these parties were would consider as a serious possibility, with a special, specific result, i.e. *E. coli* disease, which, as he later found, the parties could not at the time of contract reasonably have contemplated as a consequence. He distinguished between 'presumed contemplation' based on a special knowledge from ordinary understanding based upon general knowledge and concludes that the case falls within the latter category. He does so because he has held that the assumption, or hypothesis, to be made is that the parties had in mind at the time of contract not a breach of warranty limited to the delivery of mouldy nuts but a warranty as to the fitness of the hopper for its purpose. The assumption is of the parties asking themselves not what is likely to happen if the nuts are mouldy but what is likely to happen to the pigs if the hopper is unfit for storing nuts suitable to be fed to them. While, on his finding, nobody at the time of contract could have expected *E. coli* to ensue from eating mouldy nuts, he is clearly – and, as a matter of common sense, rightly – saying that people would contemplate, upon the second assumption, the serious possibility of injury and even death among the pigs.

And so the question becomes: was he right to make the assumption he did? In my judgement, he was: see *Grant* v. *Australian Knitting Mills Ltd* [1936] A.C. 85, and particularly the well-known passage in the speech of Lord Wright at pp. 97-100.

I would agree with *McGregor on Damages*, 13th ed. (1972), pp. 131-132 that

> '. . . in contract as in tort, it should suffice that, if physical injury or damage is within the contemplation of the parties, recovery is not to be limited because the degree of physical injury or damage could not have been anticipated.'

This is so, in my judgement, but because there is, or ought to be, a specific rule of law governing cases of physical injury but because it would be absurd to regulate damages in such cases upon the necessity of supporting the parties had a prophetic foresight as to the exact nature of the injury that does in fact arise. It is enough that upon the hypothesis predicated physical injury must have been a serious possibility. Though in loss of market or loss of profit cases the factual analysis will be very difficult from cases of physical injury, the same principles, in my judgement, apply. Given the situation of the parties at the time of contract, was the loss of profit, or market, a serious possibility, something that would have been in their minds had they contemplated breach?

It does not matter, in my judgement, if they thought that the chance of physical injury, loss of profit, loss of market, or other loss as the case may be, was slight, or that the odds were against it, provided they contemplated as a serious possibility the type of consequence, not necessarily the specific consequence, that ensued upon breach. Making the assumption as to breach that the judge did, no more than common sense was needed for them to appreciate that food affected by bad storage conditions might well cause illness in the pigs fed upon it.

As I read this judgment under appeal, this was how the judge, whose handling of the issues at trial was such that none save one survives for our consideration, reached this decision. In my judgement, he was right, upon the facts as found, to apply the first rule in *Hadley* v. *Baxendale*, 9 Exch. 341 or, if the case be one of breach of warranty, as I think it is, the rule in section 53(2) of the Sale of Goods Act 1893 without enquiring as to whether, upon a juridical analysis, the rule is based upon a presumed contemplation. At the beginning of a long and complex dispute the judge allowed common sense to prevail. I would dismiss the appeal.

Note

Orr L.J. concurred with Scarman L.J., Lord Denning M.R. would, however, have limited the plaintiffs' recourse to the loss resulting from the *physical* damage to the pigs, and not allowed them to recover the loss of profits. He argued that the defendants would be liable for physical damage even if it were *foreseen* as a *slight* possibility, but would be liable for the loss of profits if that were *contemplated* as a *serious* possibility. This distinction found no favour with Scarman and Orr L.JJ. All three judges agreed, however, in the present case, although the plaintiffs' cause of action could be framed in contract or tort, the recovery should be the same whichever form was used.

(3) SELLER'S ACTION FOR THE PRICE

It has already been pointed out that the action for the price (s. 49) has the equivalent effect that an order for specific delivery against a seller would have. Yet the latter order is rarely made. This may seem one-sided, but it will appear even more so when it is realised that giving the seller such an extensive right to sue for the price can result in a buyer carrying a greater loss than would be the case if the seller were under a duty to mitigate it by attempting in the first place to resell the goods and recover any difference between the resale price and contract price from the buyer. The reason for this is that the seller will usually be in the business of selling such goods, and is more likely to secure a favourable sale than a buyer who may not be in the business of selling such goods and is compelled to dispose of the unwanted goods for what he can get. For this reason 2-709(1)(b) of the Uniform Commercial Code (1978 text) permits the seller to recover the price only if he is 'unable after a reasonable effort to resell them at a reasonable price or the circumstances indicate that such effort will be unavailing'.

(4) THE UNPAID SELLER'S REMEDIES AGAINST THE GOODS

An unpaid seller has four remedies against the goods. These are set out in s. 39. He has a lien, a right of stoppage in transit, a right of resale and a right to withhold delivery where property in the goods has not passed to the buyer (see also s. 28). The exercise of these rights is governed by ss. 41-8. It is the right of resale which usually causes most difficulty. Until delivery to the buyer the seller obviously can sell the goods to third parties. Whether or not the third party gets a good title will depend on whether or not the property has passed to the buyer or a *nemo dat* exception applies. Whether the seller has a *right* to sell is another matter.

The seller has the *right* to sell goods to a third party:

(a) If they are unascertained, so that property in them has not passed;
(b) If the buyer repudiates, but mere late payment by him will not generally amount to a repudiation (s. 10(1));
(c) If the right is expressly reserved by the contract (s. 48(4));
(d) If the goods are perishable, *or* the seller gives notice of his intention to sell to the buyer (s. 48(3)).

Only s. 48(4) provides that a resale effects a rescission. The apparent effect is that if the seller resells under s. 48(3), after property has passed, the buyer must still pay the price of the goods (s. 49), less of course the amount of the resale. This problem was ingeniously resolved in the following case.

WARD v. BIGNALL [1967] 1 Q.B. 534 (C.A.)

The buyer agreed to purchase two used cars, a Ford Zodiac and a Standard Vanguard for £850. Before delivery, the buyer repudiated. The seller resold the Vanguard for £350, and claimed from the buyer the balance of the price as follows:

		£850
Less	deposit paid by buyer £25 resale of Vanguard £350	375
		475
Plus	advertising expenses	22 10s
		£497 10s

If the exercise of the seller's right of resale under s. 48(3) had not rescinded the contract, the buyer would *prima facie* appear to be liable for the balance of the price.

DIPLOCK L.J.
Whether or not the property had passed on May 6, 1965, the seller was only liable to deliver upon payment or tender of the balance of the purchase price (see the Sale of Goods Act, s. 28) and was entitled until then to retain possession, either by virtue of his lien as an unpaid seller if the property had passed (Sale of Goods Act, s. 39(1), or by virtue of his right to withhold delivery if the property had not passed (subs. (2) of the same section). In either case, the unpaid seller has a right to resell the goods if he gives notice of his intention to do so and the buyer does not within a reasonable time pay or tender the price (Sale of Goods Act, s. 48(3)). The note in the current edition of Chalmers that the right of resale only arises where the seller exercises his right of lien or stoppage in transitu, that is, where the property has passed to the buyer, is in my view wrong. This subsection enables a seller in possession of the goods to make time of payment of the purchase price of the essence of the contract whether the property has passed or not. The seller cannot have greater rights of resale if the property has already passed to the buyer than those which he would have if the property had remained in him.

Rescission of a contract discharges both parties from any further liability to perform their respective primary obligations under the contract, that is to say, to do thereafter those things which by their contract they had stipulated they would do. Where rescission occurs as a result of one party exercising his right to treat a breach by the other party of a stipulation in the contract as a repudiation of the contract, this gives rise to a secondary obligation of the party in breach to compensate the other party for the loss occasioned to him as a consequence of the rescission, and this secondary obligation is enforceable in an action for damages. Until, however, there is rescission by acceptance of the repudiation, the liability of both parties to perform their primary obligations under the contract continues. Thus, under a contract for the sale of goods which has not been rescinded, the seller remains liable to transfer the property in the goods to the buyer and to deliver possession of them to him until he has discharged those obligations by performing them, and the buyer remains correspondingly liable to pay for the goods and to accept possession of them.

The election by a party not in default to exercise his right of rescission by treating the contract as repudiated may be evinced by words or by conduct. Any act which puts it out of his power to perform thereafter his primary obligations under the contract, if it is an act which he is entitled to do without notice to the party in default, must amount to an election to rescind the contract. If it is an act which he is not entitled to do, it will amount to a wrongful repudiation of the contract on his part which the other party can in turn elect to treat as rescinding the contract.

Part IV of the Sale of Goods Act, section 38 to 48, deals with the rights of an unpaid seller both before the property in the goods has passed to the buyer and after it has passed. The mere fact that a seller is unpaid does not necessarily mean that the buyer is in breach of the contract, or, if he is, that his breach is one which entitles the seller to exercise his right to treat the contract as repudiated. Section 39(1) and (2) states what the unpaid seller's rights are in relation to the possession of the goods before and after the property has passed to the buyer. Subsection (1)(c) is not conduct by him which entitles the unpaid seller to treat the contract as repudiated. He remains liable to deliver the goods to the buyer upon tender of the contract price (Sale of Goods Act, s. 28). Apart from this subsection, if the unpaid seller resold the goods before or after the property had passed to the original buyer, he would remain liable to the original buyer for damages for non-delivery if the original buyer tendered the purchase price after the resale, and if the property had already passed to the original buyer at the time of the resale he would be liable to an alternative action by the original buyer for damages for conversion. The purpose of the subsection is to make time of payment of the essence of the contract whenever the goods are of a perishable nature, and to enable an unpaid seller, whatever the nature of the goods, to make payment within a reasonable time after notice of the essence of the contract. As already pointed out, an unpaid seller who resells the goods before the property has passed puts it out of his power to perform his primary obligation to the buyer to transfer the property in the goods to the buyer and, whether or not the property has already passed, to deliver up possession of the goods to the buyer. By making the act of resale one which the unpaid seller is entitled to perform, the subsection empowers the seller by his conduct in doing that act to exercise his right to treat the contract as repudiated by the buyer, that is, as rescinded, with the consequence that the buyer is discharged from any further liability to perform his primary obligation to pay the purchase price, and becomes subject to the secondary obligation to pay damages for non-acceptance of the goods. If the contract were not rescinded by the resale the seller would still be entitled to bring an action against the buyer for the price of the goods although, no doubt, he would have to credit the buyer with the proceeds of the resale. If that were the intention of the subsection one would have expected it to provide this in express terms. That it was not the intention is, however, apparent from the words used to define the remedy of the unpaid seller who has exercised his right of resale, videlicet, to 'recover from the original buyer damages for any loss occasioned by his breach of contract.' It is, of course, well-established that where a contract for the sale of goods is rescinded after the property in the goods has passed to the buyer the rescission divests the buyer of his property in the goods.

Subsection (4) deals with the consequences of a resale by a seller, not necessarily an 'unpaid seller' as defined in section 38, made in the exercise of an express right of resale reserved in the contract on the buyer making default. If such an express right were exercisable after the property in the goods had passed to the buyer, its exercise might, on one view, be regarded as an alternative mode of performance of the seller's primary obligations under the contract, and the resale as being made by the seller as agent for the buyer. It was, therefore, necessary to provide expressly that the exercise of an express power of resale should rescind the original contract of sale. That is, in my view, the explanation of the express reference to rescission in subsection (4). The absence of a similar express reference to rescission in subsection (3) is no sufficient ground for ascribing to subsection (3) a meaning which the actual words of the subsection would appear to contradict and which would, in my view, conflict with the general principles of the law of contract.

In the present case the unpaid seller only resold part of the goods which he had contracted to sell to the original buyer. This makes no difference, however. His primary duty under the contract was to deliver both cars to the buyer. If he delivered only one, the buyer would be entitled to reject it (Sale of Goods Act, s. 30(1)). By his conduct in selling the Vanguard on May 24, 1965, the unpaid seller put it out of his power to perform his primary obligation under the contract. He thereby elected to treat the contract as rescinded. The property in the Zodiac thereupon reverted to him, and his only remedy against the buyer after May 24, 1965, was for damages for non-acceptance of the two cars, of which the *prima facie* measure is the difference between the contract price and their market value on May 24, 1965.

I, too, would allow this appeal, and enter judgment for the plaintiffs for £47 10s instead of £497 10s.

7 Exclusion of Liability

The possibility of excluding the liability imposed on sellers under ss. 12-15 of the Sale of Goods Act was restricted by the Supply of Goods (Implied Terms) Act 1973. This Act supplemented a number of devices invented by the courts for controlling exemption clauses, some of them of doubtful authority. The Unfair Contract Terms Act 1977 now regulates the exclusion of liability in sales contracts (as well as the exclusion of negligence liability and contract liability generally). By s. 6(1) liability under the seller's title warranties in s. 12 cannot be excluded. Liability under the description and quality warranties contained in ss. 13-15 cannot be excluded either, but only as against a person 'dealing as a consumer' (which term is defined in s. 12). Against other persons such liability can be excluded provided the term satisfies the Act's requirement of reasonableness (s. 11(2)). Guidelines for the application of this reasonableness test are set out in Schedule 2.

Attempts to exclude liability for defective goods or negligence by the terms of so-called 'guarantees' of consumer goods is regulated by s. 5 of the Act. What is meant by 'guarantee' in this context is the common sort of manufacturer's assurance that defects in the product will be made good (s. 5(2)(b)). S. 5 relates to the manufacturer's own liability. The liability of the actual seller, usually a shop, is regulated *inter alia* by s. 6 mentioned above. Of course, there is a basic contract problem here: there is no privity of contract between the manufacturer and the customer, and arguably the manufacturer's only liability to the customer is therefore in tort anyway. The argument that the customer by posting off the 'guarantee' to the manufacturer accepts an offer made by the manufacturer under which the customer, in consideration of surrendering his common law rights against the manufacturer, has conferred on him the rights set out in the 'guarantee', now founders on the fact that the customer cannot now surrender his rights to the extent that the Act prevents this.

The sections of the Act which regulate the exclusion of liability for negligence, breach of contract generally and misrepresentation (ss. 2, 3, and 8) may also be relevant in disputes involving sales of goods. For reasons of space, however, it was thought appropriate to omit them

DOI: 10.4324/9781003174615-8

from a specific guide of this sort.[94] In contracts analogous to sales, i.e. contracts under which ownership of goods passes, but which are not sales or hire purchase transactions, s. 7(1) provides that ss. 2-4 of the Act apply to terms excluding or restricting liability. S. 7(2) provides that as against a person dealing as consumer, liability for correspondence with description or sample cannot be excluded, nor liability for quality or fitness, and as against other persons s. 7(3) provides that the exclusion must satisfy the requirement of reasonableness (the guidelines are again those set out in Schedule 2).

For the purpose of clauses which do not seek to exclude liability altogether, but only to limit the damages recoverable to a certain amount, 6 and 7 apply in the same way, i.e. such clauses will be inoperative against a person dealing as consumer, and in other cases must satisfy the requirement of reasonableness. In the latter case, however, s. 11(4) requires regard to be had to the financial resources available to the profferor and possibility of insurance cover, as well as the guidelines in Schedule 2. S. 5 also applies to limitation of damages clauses.

8 Statutes

SALE OF GOODS ACT 1979 (C. 54)

1979 CHAPTER 54

An Act to consolidate the law relating to the sale of goods. [6th December 1979]

BE IT ENACTED by the Queen's most Excellent Majesty, by and with the advice and consent of the Lords Spiritual and Temporal, and Commons, in this present Parliament assembled, and by the authority of the same, as follows:—

PART I

CONTRACTS TO WHICH ACT APPLIES

Contracts to which Act applies.

1.—(1) This Act applies to contracts of sale of goods made on or after (but not to those made before) 1 January 1894.

(2) In relation to contracts made on certain dates, this Act applies subject to the modification of certain of its sections as mentioned in Schedule 1 below.

(3) Any such modification is indicated in the section concerned by a reference to Schedule 1 below.

(4) Accordingly, where a section does not contain such a reference, this Act applies in relation to the contract concerned without such modification of the section.

PART II

FORMATION OF THE CONTRACT

Contract of sale

Contract of sale.

2.—(1) A contract of sale of goods is a contract by which the seller transfers or agrees to transfer the property in goods to the buyer for a money consideration, called the price.

A 2

DOI: 10.4324/9781003174615-9

PART II

(2) There may be a contract of sale between one part owner and another.

(3) A contract of sale may be absolute or conditional.

(4) Where under a contract of sale the property in the goods is transferred from the seller to the buyer the contract is called a sale.

(5) Where under a contract of sale the transfer of the property in the goods is to take place at a future time or subject to some condition later to be fulfilled the contract is called an agreement to sell.

(6) An agreement to sell becomes a sale when the time elapses or the conditions are fulfilled subject to which the property in the goods is to be transferred.

Capacity to buy and sell.

3.—(1) Capacity to buy and sell is regulated by the general law concerning capacity to contract and to transfer and acquire property.

(2) Where necessaries are sold and delivered to a minor or to a person who by reason of mental incapacity or drunkenness is incompetent to contract, he must pay a reasonable price for them.

(3) In subsection (2) above " necessaries " means goods suitable to the condition in life of the minor or other person concerned and to his actual requirements at the time of the sale and delivery.

Formalities of contract

How contract of sale is made.

4.—(1) Subject to this and any other Act, a contract of sale may be made in writing (either with or without seal), or by word of mouth, or partly in writing and partly by word of mouth, or may be implied from the conduct of the parties.

(2) Nothing in this section affects the law relating to corporations.

Subject matter of contract

Existing or future goods.

5.—(1) The goods which form the subject of a contract of sale may be either existing goods, owned or possessed by the seller, or goods to be manufactured or acquired by him after the making of the contract of sale, in this Act called future goods.

(2) There may be a contract for the sale of goods the acquisition of which by the seller depends on a contingency which may or may not happen.

(3) Where by a contract of sale the seller purports to effect a present sale of future goods, the contract operates as an agreement to sell the goods. **Part II**

6. Where there is a contract for the sale of specific goods, and the goods without the knowledge of the seller have perished at the time when the contract is made, the contract is void. Goods which have perished.

7. Where there is an agreement to sell specific goods and subsequently the goods, without any fault on the part of the seller or buyer, perish before the risk passes to the buyer, the agreement is avoided. Goods perishing before sale but after agreement to sell.

The price

8.—(1) The price in a contract of sale may be fixed by the contract, or may be left to be fixed in a manner agreed by the contract, or may be determined by the course of dealing between the parties. Ascertainment of price.

(2) Where the price is not determined as mentioned in subsection (1) above the buyer must pay a reasonable price.

(3) What is a reasonable price is a question of fact dependent on the circumstances of each particular case.

9.—(1) Where there is an agreement to sell goods on the terms that the price is to be fixed by the valuation of a third party, and he cannot or does not make the valuation, the agreement is avoided; but if the goods or any part of them have been delivered to and appropriated by the buyer he must pay a reasonable price for them. Agreement to sell at valuation.

(2) Where the third party is prevented from making the valuation by the fault of the seller or buyer, the party not at fault may maintain an action for damages against the party at fault.

Conditions and warranties

10.—(1) Unless a different intention appears from the terms of the contract, stipulations as to time of payment are not of the essence of a contract of sale. Stipulations about time.

(2) Whether any other stipulation as to time is or is not of the essence of the contract depends on the terms of the contract.

(3) In a contract of sale " month " prima facie means calendar month.

PART II

When condition to be treated as warranty.

11.—(1) Subsections (2) to (4) and (7) below do not apply to Scotland and subsection (5) below applies only to Scotland.

(2) Where a contract of sale is subject to a condition to be fulfilled by the seller, the buyer may waive the condition, or may elect to treat the breach of the condition as a breach of warranty and not as a ground for treating the contract as repudiated.

(3) Whether a stipulation in a contract of sale is a condition, the breach of which may give rise to a right to treat the contract as repudiated, or a warranty, the breach of which may give rise to a claim for damages but not to a right to reject the goods and treat the contract as repudiated, depends in each case on the construction of the contract; and a stipulation may be a condition, though called a warranty in the contract.

(4) Where a contract of sale is not severable and the buyer has accepted the goods or part of them, the breach of a condition to be fulfilled by the seller can only be treated as a breach of warranty, and not as a ground for rejecting the goods and treating the contract as repudiated, unless there is an express or implied term of the contract to that effect.

(5) In Scotland, failure by the seller to perform any material part of a contract of sale is a breach of contract, which entitles the buyer either within a reasonable time after delivery to reject the goods and treat the contract as repudiated, or to retain the goods and treat the failure to perform such material part as a breach which may give rise to a claim for compensation or damages.

(6) Nothing in this section affects a condition or warranty whose fulfilment is excused by law by reason of impossibility or otherwise.

(7) Paragraph 2 of Schedule 1 below applies in relation to a contract made before 22 April 1967 or (in the application of this Act to Northern Ireland) 28 July 1967.

Implied terms about title, etc.

12.—(1) In a contract of sale, other than one to which subsection (3) below applies, there is an implied condition on the part of the seller that in the case of a sale he has a right to sell the goods, and in the case of an agreement to sell he will have such a right at the time when the property is to pass.

(2) In a contract of sale, other than one to which subsection (3) below applies, there is also an implied warranty that—

(*a*) the goods are free, and will remain free until the time when the property is to pass, from any charge or encumbrance not disclosed or known to the buyer before the contract is made, and

PART II

(*b*) the buyer will enjoy quiet possession of the goods except so far as it may be disturbed by the owner or other person entitled to the benefit of any charge or encumbrance so disclosed or known.

(3) This subsection applies to a contract of sale in the case of which there appears from the contract or is to be inferred from its circumstances an intention that the seller should transfer only such title as he or a third person may have.

(4) In a contract to which subsection (3) above applies there is an implied warranty that all charges or encumbrances known to the seller and not known to the buyer have been disclosed to the buyer before the contract is made.

(5) In a contract to which subsection (3) above applies there is also an implied warranty that none of the following will disturb the buyer's quiet possession of the goods, namely—

(*a*) the seller;

(*b*) in a case where the parties to the contract intend that the seller should transfer only such title as a third person may have, that person;

(*c*) anyone claiming through or under the seller or that third person otherwise than under a charge or encumbrance disclosed or known to the buyer before the contract is made.

(6) Paragraph 3 of Schedule 1 below applies in relation to a contract made before 18 May 1973.

Sale by description.

13.—(1) Where there is a contract for the sale of goods by description, there is an implied condition that the goods will correspond with the description.

(2) If the sale is by sample as well as by description it is not sufficient that the bulk of the goods corresponds with the sample if the goods do not also correspond with the description.

(3) A sale of goods is not prevented from being a sale by description by reason only that, being exposed for sale or hire, they are selected by the buyer.

(4) Paragraph 4 of Schedule 1 below applies in relation to a contract made before 18 May 1973.

Implied terms about quality or fitness.

14.—(1) Except as provided by this section and section 15 below and subject to any other enactment, there is no implied condition or warranty about the quality or fitness for any particular purpose of goods supplied under a contract of sale.

(2) Where the seller sells goods in the course of a business, there is an implied condition that the goods supplied under the

PART II contract are of merchantable quality, except that there is no such condition—

(*a*) as regards defects specifically drawn to the buyer's attention before the contract is made; or

(*b*) if the buyer examines the goods before the contract is made, as regards defects which that examination ought to reveal.

(3) Where the seller sells goods in the course of a business and the buyer, expressly or by implication, makes known—

(*a*) to the seller, or

(*b*) where the purchase price or part of it is payable by instalments and the goods were previously sold by a credit-broker to the seller, to that credit-broker,

any particular purpose for which the goods are being bought, there is an implied condition that the goods supplied under the contract are reasonably fit for that purpose, whether or not that is a purpose for which such goods are commonly supplied, except where the circumstances show that the buyer does not rely, or that it is unreasonable for him to rely, on the skill or judgment of the seller or credit-broker.

(4) An implied condition or warranty about quality or fitness for a particular purpose may be annexed to a contract of sale by usage.

(5) The preceding provisions of this section apply to a sale by a person who in the course of a business is acting as agent for another as they apply to a sale by a principal in the course of a business, except where that other is not selling in the course of a business and either the buyer knows that fact or reasonable steps are taken to bring it to the notice of the buyer before the contract is made.

(6) Goods of any kind are of merchantable quality within the meaning of subsection (2) above if they are as fit for the purpose or purposes for which goods of that kind are commonly bought as it is reasonable to expect having regard to any description applied to them, the price (if relevant) and all the other relevant circumstances.

(7) Paragraph 5 of Schedule 1 below applies in relation to a contract made on or after 18 May 1973 and before the appointed day, and paragraph 6 in relation to one made before 18 May 1973.

(8) In subsection (7) above and paragraph 5 of Schedule 1 below references to the appointed day are to the day appointed for the purposes of those provisions by an order of the Secretary of State made by statutory instrument.

Sale by sample

PART II

15.—(1) A contract of sale is a contract for sale by sample where there is an express or implied term to that effect in the contract. Sale by sample.

(2) In the case of a contract for sale by sample there is an implied condition—

(*a*) that the bulk will correspond with the sample in quality;

(*b*) that the buyer will have a reasonable opportunity of comparing the bulk with the sample;

(*c*) that the goods will be free from any defect, rendering them unmerchantable, which would not be apparent on reasonable examination of the sample.

(3) In subsection (2)(*c*) above "unmerchantable" is to be construed in accordance with section 14(6) above.

(4) Paragraph 7 of Schedule 1 below applies in relation to a contract made before 18 May 1973.

PART III

EFFECTS OF THE CONTRACT

Transfer of property as between seller and buyer

16. Where there is a contract for the sale of unascertained goods no property in the goods is transferred to the buyer unless and until the goods are ascertained. Goods must be ascertained.

17.—(1) Where there is a contract for the sale of specific or ascertained goods the property in them is transferred to the buyer at such time as the parties to the contract intend it to be transferred. Property passes when intended to pass.

(2) For the purpose of ascertaining the intention of the parties regard shall be had to the terms of the contract, the conduct of the parties and the circumstances of the case.

18. Unless a different intention appears, the following are rules for ascertaining the intention of the parties as to the time at which the property in the goods is to pass to the buyer. Rules for ascertaining intention.

Rule 1.—Where there is an unconditional contract for the sale of specific goods in a deliverable state the property in the goods passes to the buyer when the contract is made, and it is immaterial whether the time of payment or the time of delivery, or both, be postponed.

Rule 2.—Where there is a contract for the sale of specific goods and the seller is bound to do something to the goods for the purpose of putting them into a deliverable state, the property does not pass until the thing is done and the buyer has notice that it has been done.

PART III

Rule 3.—Where there is a contract for the sale of specific goods in a deliverable state but the seller is bound to weigh, measure, test, or do some other act or thing with reference to the goods for the purpose of ascertaining the price, the property does not pass until the act or thing is done and the buyer has notice that it has been done.

Rule 4.—When goods are delivered to the buyer on approval or on sale or return or other similar terms the property in the goods passes to the buyer:—

(*a*) when he signifies his approval or acceptance to the seller or does any other act adopting the transaction;

(*b*) if he does not signify his approval or acceptance to the seller but retains the goods without giving notice of rejection, then, if a time has been fixed for the return of the goods, on the expiration of that time, and, if no time has been fixed, on the expiration of a reasonable time.

Rule 5.—(1) Where there is a contract for the sale of unascertained or future goods by description, and goods of that description and in a deliverable state are unconditionally appropriated to the contract, either by the seller with the assent of the buyer or by the buyer with the assent of the seller, the property in the goods then passes to the buyer; and the assent may be express or implied, and may be given either before or after the appropriation is made.

(2) Where, in pursuance of the contract, the seller delivers the goods to the buyer or to a carrier or other bailee or custodier (whether named by the buyer or not) for the purpose of transmission to the buyer, and does not reserve the right of disposal, he is to be taken to have unconditionally appropriated the goods to the contract.

Reservation of right of disposal.

19.—(1) Where there is a contract for the sale of specific goods or where goods are subsequently appropriated to the contract, the seller may, by the terms of the contract or appropriation, reserve the right of disposal of the goods until certain conditions are fulfilled; and in such a case, notwithstanding the delivery of the goods to the buyer, or to a carrier or other bailee or custodier for the purpose of transmission to the buyer, the property in the goods does not pass to the buyer until the conditions imposed by the seller are fulfilled.

(2) Where goods are shipped, and by the bill of lading the goods are deliverable to the order of the seller or his agent, the seller is prima facie to be taken to reserve the right of disposal.

(3) Where the seller of goods draws on the buyer for the price, and transmits the bill of exchange and bill of lading to the buyer together to secure acceptance or payment of the bill of exchange, the buyer is bound to return the bill of lading if he does not honour the bill of exchange, and if he wrongfully retains the bill of lading the property in the goods does not pass to him.

Risk prima facie passes with property.

20.—(1) Unless otherwise agreed, the goods remain at the seller's risk until the property in them is transferred to the buyer, but when the property in them is transferred to the buyer the goods are at the buyer's risk whether delivery has been made or not.

(2) But where delivery has been delayed through the fault of either buyer or seller the goods are at the risk of the party at fault as regards any loss which might not have occurred but for such fault.

(3) Nothing in this section affects the duties or liabilities of either seller or buyer as a bailee or custodier of the goods of the other party.

Transfer of title

Sale by person not the owner.

21.—(1) Subject to this Act, where goods are sold by a person who is not their owner, and who does not sell them under the authority or with the consent of the owner, the buyer acquires no better title to the goods than the seller had, unless the owner of the goods is by his conduct precluded from denying the seller's authority to sell.

(2) Nothing in this Act affects—

(*a*) the provisions of the Factors Acts or any enactment enabling the apparent owner of goods to dispose of them as if he were their true owner;

(*b*) the validity of any contract of sale under any special common law or statutory power of sale or under the order of a court of competent jurisdiction.

Market overt.

22.—(1) Where goods are sold in market overt, according to the usage of the market, the buyer acquires a good title to the goods, provided he buys them in good faith and without notice of any defect or want of title on the part of the seller.

(2) This section does not apply to Scotland.

(3) Paragraph 8 of Schedule 1 below applies in relation to a contract under which goods were sold before 1 January 1968 or (in the application of this Act to Northern Ireland) 29 August 1967.

PART III

Sale under voidable title.

23. When the seller of goods has a voidable title to them, but his title has not been avoided at the time of the sale, the buyer acquires a good title to the goods, provided he buys them in good faith and without notice of the seller's defect of title.

Seller in possession after sale.

24. Where a person having sold goods continues or is in possession of the goods, or of the documents of title to the goods, the delivery or transfer by that person, or by a mercantile agent acting for him, of the goods or documents of title under any sale, pledge, or other disposition thereof, to any person receiving the same in good faith and without notice of the previous sale, has the same effect as if the person making the delivery or transfer were expressly authorised by the owner of the goods to make the same.

Buyer in possession after sale.

25.—(1) Where a person having bought or agreed to buy goods obtains, with the consent of the seller, possession of the goods or the documents of title to the goods, the delivery or transfer by that person, or by a mercantile agent acting for him, of the goods or documents of title, under any sale, pledge, or other disposition thereof, to any person receiving the same in good faith and without notice of any lien or other right of the original seller in respect of the goods, has the same effect as if the person making the delivery or transfer were a mercantile agent in possession of the goods or documents of title with the consent of the owner.

(2) For the purposes of subsection (1) above—

(*a*) the buyer under a conditional sale agreement is to be taken not to be a person who has bought or agreed to buy goods, and

(*b*) " conditional sale agreement " means an agreement for the sale of goods which is a consumer credit agreement within the meaning of the Consumer Credit Act 1974 under which the purchase price or part of it is payable by instalments, and the property in the goods is to remain in the seller (notwithstanding that the buyer is to be in possession of the goods) until such conditions as to the payment of instalments or otherwise as may be specified in the agreement are fulfilled.

1974 c. 39.

(3) Paragraph 9 of Schedule 1 below applies in relation to a contract under which a person buys or agrees to buy goods and which is made before the appointed day.

(4) In subsection (3) above and paragraph 9 of Schedule 1 below references to the appointed day are to the day appointed for the purposes of those provisions by an order of the Secretary of State made by statutory instrument.

26. In sections 24 and 25 above " mercantile agent " means a mercantile agent having in the customary course of his business as such agent authority either—

PART III Supplementary to sections 24 and 25.

(*a*) to sell goods, or

(*b*) to consign goods for the purpose of sale, or

(*c*) to buy goods, or

(*d*) to raise money on the security of goods.

PART IV

PERFORMANCE OF THE CONTRACT

27. It is the duty of the seller to deliver the goods, and of the buyer to accept and pay for them, in accordance with the terms of the contract of sale.

Duties of seller and buyer.

28. Unless otherwise agreed, delivery of the goods and payment of the price are concurrent conditions, that is to say, the seller must be ready and willing to give possession of the goods to the buyer in exchange for the price and the buyer must be ready and willing to pay the price in exchange for possession of the goods.

Payment and delivery are concurrent conditions.

29.—(1) Whether it is for the buyer to take possession of the goods or for the seller to send them to the buyer is a question depending in each case on the contract, express or implied, between the parties.

Rules about delivery.

(2) Apart from any such contract, express or implied, the place of delivery is the seller's place of business if he has one, and if not, his residence; except that, if the contract is for the sale of specific goods, which to the knowledge of the parties when the contract is made are in some other place, then that place is the place of delivery.

(3) Where under the contract of sale the seller is bound to send the goods to the buyer, but no time for sending them is fixed, the seller is bound to send them within a reasonable time.

(4) Where the goods at the time of sale are in the possession of a third person, there is no delivery by seller to buyer unless and until the third person acknowledges to the buyer that he holds the goods on his behalf; but nothing in this section affects the operation of the issue or transfer of any document of title to goods.

(5) Demand or tender of delivery may be treated as ineffectual unless made at a reasonable hour; and what is a reasonable hour is a question of fact.

(6) Unless otherwise agreed, the expenses of and incidental to putting the goods into a deliverable state must be borne by the seller.

Delivery of wrong quantity.

30.—(1) Where the seller delivers to the buyer a quantity of goods less than he contracted to sell, the buyer may reject them, but if the buyer accepts the goods so delivered he must pay for them at the contract rate.

(2) Where the seller delivers to the buyer a quantity of goods larger than he contracted to sell, the buyer may accept the goods included in the contract and reject the rest, or he may reject the whole.

(3) Where the seller delivers to the buyer a quantity of goods larger than he contracted to sell and the buyer accepts the whole of the goods so delivered he must pay for them at the contract rate.

(4) Where the seller delivers to the buyer the goods he contracted to sell mixed with goods of a different description not included in the contract, the buyer may accept the goods which are in accordance with the contract and reject the rest, or he may reject the whole.

(5) This section is subject to any usage of trade, special agreement, or course of dealing between the parties.

Instalment deliveries.

31.—(1) Unless otherwise agreed, the buyer of goods is not bound to accept delivery of them by instalments.

(2) Where there is a contract for the sale of goods to be delivered by stated instalments, which are to be separately paid for, and the seller makes defective deliveries in respect of one or more instalments, or the buyer neglects or refuses to take delivery of or pay for one or more instalments, it is a question in each case depending on the terms of the contract and the circumstances of the case whether the breach of contract is a repudiation of the whole contract or whether it is a severable breach giving rise to a claim for compensation but not to a right to treat the whole contract as repudiated.

Delivery to carrier.

32.—(1) Where, in pursuance of a contract of sale, the seller is authorised or required to send the goods to the buyer, delivery of the goods to a carrier (whether named by the buyer or not) for the purpose of transmission to the buyer is prima facie deemed to be a delivery of the goods to the buyer.

(2) Unless otherwise authorised by the buyer, the seller must make such contract with the carrier on behalf of the buyer as may be reasonable having regard to the nature of the goods and the other circumstances of the case; and if the seller omits to do

so, and the goods are lost or damaged in course of transit, the buyer may decline to treat the delivery to the carrier as a delivery to himself or may hold the seller responsible in damages.

(3) Unless otherwise agreed, where goods are sent by the seller to the buyer by a route involving sea transit, under circumstances in which it is usual to insure, the seller must give such notice to the buyer as may enable him to insure them during their sea transit; and if the seller fails to do so, the goods are at his risk during such sea transit.

Risk where goods are delivered at distant place.

33. Where the seller of goods agrees to deliver them at his own risk at a place other than that where they are when sold, the buyer must nevertheless (unless otherwise agreed) take any risk of deterioration in the goods necessarily incident to the course of transit.

Buyer's right of examining the goods.

34.—(1) Where goods are delivered to the buyer, and he has not previously examined them, he is not deemed to have accepted them until he has had a reasonable opportunity of examining them for the purpose of ascertaining whether they are in conformity with the contract.

(2) Unless otherwise agreed, when the seller tenders delivery of goods to the buyer, he is bound on request to afford the buyer a reasonable opportunity of examining the goods for the purpose of ascertaining whether they are in conformity with the contract.

Acceptance.

35.—(1) The buyer is deemed to have accepted the goods when he intimates to the seller that he has accepted them, or (except where section 34 above otherwise provides) when the goods have been delivered to him and he does any act in relation to them which is inconsistent with the ownership of the seller, or when after the lapse of a reasonable time he retains the goods without intimating to the seller that he has rejected them.

(2) Paragraph 10 of Schedule 1 below applies in relation to a contract made before 22 April 1967 or (in the application of this Act to Northern Ireland) 28 July 1967.

Buyer not bound to return rejected goods.

36. Unless otherwise agreed, where goods are delivered to the buyer, and he refuses to accept them, having the right to do so, he is not bound to return them to the seller, but it is sufficient if he intimates to the seller that he refuses to accept them.

Buyer's liability for not taking delivery of goods.

37.—(1) When the seller is ready and willing to deliver the goods, and requests the buyer to take delivery, and the buyer does not within a reasonable time after such request take delivery of the goods, he is liable to the seller for any loss occasioned by his neglect or refusal to take delivery, and also for a reasonable charge for the care and custody of the goods.

(2) Nothing in this section affects the rights of the seller where the neglect or refusal of the buyer to take delivery amounts to a repudiation of the contract.

PART V

RIGHTS OF UNPAID SELLER AGAINST THE GOODS

Preliminary

Unpaid seller defined.

38.—(1) The seller of goods is an unpaid seller within the meaning of this Act—

(*a*) when the whole of the price has not been paid or tendered ;

(*b*) when a bill of exchange or other negotiable instrument has been received as conditional payment, and the condition on which it was received has not been fulfilled by reason of the dishonour of the instrument or otherwise.

(2) In this Part of this Act " seller " includes any person who is in the position of a seller, as, for instance, an agent of the seller to whom the bill of lading has been indorsed, or a consignor or agent who has himself paid (or is directly responsible for) the price.

Unpaid seller's rights.

39.—(1) Subject to this and any other Act, notwithstanding that the property in the goods may have passed to the buyer, the unpaid seller of goods, as such, has by implication of law—

(*a*) a lien on the goods or right to retain them for the price while he is in possession of them ;

(*b*) in case of the insolvency of the buyer, a right of stopping the goods in transit after he has parted with the possession of them ;

(*c*) a right of re-sale as limited by this Act.

(2) Where the property in goods has not passed to the buyer, the unpaid seller has (in addition to his other remedies) a right of withholding delivery similar to and co-extensive with his rights of lien or retention and stoppage in transit where the property has passed to the buyer.

Attachment by seller in Scotland.

40. In Scotland a seller of goods may attach them while in his own hands or possession by arrestment or poinding ; and such arrestment or poinding shall have the same operation and effect in a competition or otherwise as an arrestment or poinding by a third party.

Unpaid seller's lien PART V

41.—(1) Subject to this Act, the unpaid seller of goods who is in possession of them is entitled to retain possession of them until payment or tender of the price in the following cases:— Seller's lien.

(*a*) where the goods have been sold without any stipulation as to credit;

(*b*) where the goods have been sold on credit but the term of credit has expired;

(*c*) where the buyer becomes insolvent.

(2) The seller may exercise his lien or right of retention notwithstanding that he is in possession of the goods as agent or bailee or custodier for the buyer.

42. Where an unpaid seller has made part delivery of the goods, he may exercise his lien or right of retention on the remainder, unless such part delivery has been made under such circumstances as to show an agreement to waive the lien or right of retention. Part delivery.

43.—(1) The unpaid seller of goods loses his lien or right of retention in respect of them— Termination of lien.

(*a*) when he delivers the goods to a carrier or other bailee or custodier for the purpose of transmission to the buyer without reserving the right of disposal of the goods;

(*b*) when the buyer or his agent lawfully obtains possession of the goods;

(*c*) by waiver of the lien or right of retention.

(2) An unpaid seller of goods who has a lien or right of retention in respect of them does not lose his lien or right of retention by reason only that he has obtained judgment or decree for the price of the goods.

Stoppage in transit

44. Subject to this Act, when the buyer of goods becomes insolvent the unpaid seller who has parted with the possession of the goods has the right of stopping them in transit, that is to say, he may resume possession of the goods as long as they are in course of transit, and may retain them until payment or tender of the price. Right of stoppage in transit.

45.—(1) Goods are deemed to be in course of transit from the time when they are delivered to a carrier or other bailee or custodier for the purpose of transmission to the buyer, until the buyer or his agent in that behalf takes delivery of them from the carrier or other bailee or custodier. Duration of transit.

PART V

(2) If the buyer or his agent in that behalf obtains delivery of the goods before their arrival at the appointed destination, the transit is at an end.

(3) If, after the arrival of the goods at the appointed destination, the carrier or other bailee or custodier acknowledges to the buyer or his agent that he holds the goods on his behalf and continues in possession of them as bailee or custodier for the buyer or his agent, the transit is at an end, and it is immaterial that a further destination for the goods may have been indicated by the buyer.

(4) If the goods are rejected by the buyer, and the carrier or other bailee or custodier continues in possession of them, the transit is not deemed to be at an end, even if the seller has refused to receive them back.

(5) When goods are delivered to a ship chartered by the buyer it is a question depending on the circumstances of the particular case whether they are in the possession of the master as a carrier or as agent to the buyer.

(6) Where the carrier or other bailee or custodier wrongfully refuses to deliver the goods to the buyer or his agent in that behalf, the transit is deemed to be at an end.

(7) Where part delivery of the goods has been made to the buyer or his agent in that behalf, the remainder of the goods may be stopped in transit, unless such part delivery has been made under such circumstances as to show an agreement to give up possession of the whole of the goods.

How stoppage in transit is effected.

46.—(1) The unpaid seller may exercise his right of stoppage in transit either by taking actual possession of the goods or by giving notice of his claim to the carrier or other bailee or custodier in whose possession the goods are.

(2) The notice may be given either to the person in actual possession of the goods or to his principal.

(3) If given to the principal, the notice is ineffective unless given at such time and under such circumstances that the principal, by the exercise of reasonable diligence, may communicate it to his servant or agent in time to prevent a delivery to the buyer.

(4) When notice of stoppage in transit is given by the seller to the carrier or other bailee or custodier in possession of the goods, he must re-deliver the goods to, or according to the directions of, the seller; and the expenses of the re-delivery must be borne by the seller.

Re-sale etc. by buyer

47.—(1) Subject to this Act, the unpaid seller's right of lien or retention or stoppage in transit is not affected by any sale or other disposition of the goods which the buyer may have made, unless the seller has assented to it.

Effect of sub-sale etc. by buyer.

(2) Where a document of title to goods has been lawfully transferred to any person as buyer or owner of the goods, and that person transfers the document to a person who takes it in good faith and for valuable consideration, then—

(*a*) if the last-mentioned transfer was by way of sale the unpaid seller's right of lien or retention or stoppage in transit is defeated ; and

(*b*) if the last-mentioned transfer was made by way of pledge or other disposition for value, the unpaid seller's right of lien or retention or stoppage in transit can only be exercised subject to the rights of the transferee.

Rescission : and re-sale by seller

48.—(1) Subject to this section, a contract of sale is not rescinded by the mere exercise by an unpaid seller of his right of lien or retention or stoppage in transit.

Rescission: and re-sale by seller.

(2) Where an unpaid seller who has exercised his right of lien or retention or stoppage in transit re-sells the goods, the buyer acquires a good title to them as against the original buyer.

(3) Where the goods are of a perishable nature, or where the unpaid seller gives notice to the buyer of his intention to re-sell, and the buyer does not within a reasonable time pay or tender the price, the unpaid seller may re-sell the goods and recover from the original buyer damages for any loss occasioned by his breach of contract.

(4) Where the seller expressly reserves the right of re-sale in case the buyer should make default, and on the buyer making default re-sells the goods, the original contract of sale is rescinded but without prejudice to any claim the seller may have for damages.

Part VI

Actions for Breach of the Contract

Seller's remedies

49.—(1) Where, under a contract of sale, the property in the goods has passed to the buyer and he wrongfully neglects or refuses to pay for the goods according to the terms of the contract, the seller may maintain an action against him for the price of the goods.

Action for price.

PART VI

(2) Where, under a contract of sale, the price is payable on a day certain irrespective of delivery and the buyer wrongfully neglects or refuses to pay such price, the seller may maintain an action for the price, although the property in the goods has not passed and the goods have not been appropriated to the contract.

(3) Nothing in this section prejudices the right of the seller in Scotland to recover interest on the price from the date of tender of the goods, or from the date on which the price was payable, as the case may be.

Damages for non-acceptance.

50.—(1) Where the buyer wrongfully neglects or refuses to accept and pay for the goods, the seller may maintain an action against him for damages for non-acceptance.

(2) The measure of damages is the estimated loss directly and naturally resulting, in the ordinary course of events, from the buyer's breach of contract.

(3) Where there is an available market for the goods in question the measure of damages is prima facie to be ascertained by the difference between the contract price and the market or current price at the time or times when the goods ought to have been accepted or (if no time was fixed for acceptance) at the time of the refusal to accept.

Buyer's remedies

Damages for non-delivery.

51.—(1) Where the seller wrongfully neglects or refuses to deliver the goods to the buyer, the buyer may maintain an action against the seller for damages for non-delivery.

(2) The measure of damages is the estimated loss directly and naturally resulting, in the ordinary course of events, from the seller's breach of contract.

(3) Where there is an available market for the goods in question the measure of damages is prima facie to be ascertained by the difference between the contract price and the market or current price of the goods at the time or times when they ought to have been delivered or (if no time was fixed) at the time of the refusal to deliver.

Specific performance.

52.—(1) In any action for breach of contract to deliver specific or ascertained goods the court may, if it thinks fit, on the plaintiff's application, by its judgment or decree direct that the contract shall be performed specifically, without giving the defendant the option of retaining the goods on payment of damages.

(2) The plaintiff's application may be made at any time before judgment or decree.

(3) The judgment or decree may be unconditional, or on such terms and conditions as to damages, payment of the price and otherwise as seem just to the court.

(4) The provisions of this section shall be deemed to be supplementary to, and not in derogation of, the right of specific implement in Scotland.

Remedy for breach of warranty.

53.—(1) Where there is a breach of warranty by the seller, or where the buyer elects (or is compelled) to treat any breach of a condition on the part of the seller as a breach of warranty, the buyer is not by reason only of such breach of warranty entitled to reject the goods ; but he may—

(*a*) set up against the seller the breach of warranty in diminution or extinction of the price, or

(*b*) maintain an action against the seller for damages for the breach of warranty.

(2) The measure of damages for breach of warranty is the estimated loss directly and naturally resulting, in the ordinary course of events, from the breach of warranty.

(3) In the case of breach of warranty of quality such loss is prima facie the difference between the value of the goods at the time of delivery to the buyer and the value they would have had if they had fulfilled the warranty.

(4) The fact that the buyer has set up the breach of warranty in diminution or extinction of the price does not prevent him from maintaining an action for the same breach of warranty if he has suffered further damage.

(5) Nothing in this section prejudices or affects the buyer's right of rejection in Scotland as declared by this Act.

Interest, etc.

Interest, etc.

54. Nothing in this Act affects the right of the buyer or the seller to recover interest or special damages in any case where by law interest or special damages may be recoverable, or to recover money paid where the consideration for the payment of it has failed.

PART VII

SUPPLEMENTARY

Exclusion of implied terms.

1977 c. 50.

55.—(1) Where a right, duty or liability would arise under a contract of sale of goods by implication of law, it may (subject to the Unfair Contract Terms Act 1977) be negatived or varied by express agreement, or by the course of dealing between the parties, or by such usage as binds both parties to the contract.

PART VII

(2) An express condition or warranty does not negative a condition or warranty implied by this Act unless inconsistent with it.

(3) Paragraph 11 of Schedule 1 below applies in relation to a contract made on or after 18 May 1973 and before 1 February 1978, and paragraph 12 in relation to one made before 18 May 1973.

Conflict of laws.

56. Paragraph 13 of Schedule 1 below applies in relation to a contract made on or after 18 May 1973 and before 1 February 1978, so as to make provision about conflict of laws in relation to such a contract.

Auction sales.

57.—(1) Where goods are put up for sale by auction in lots, each lot is prima facie deemed to be the subject of a separate contract of sale.

(2) A sale by auction is complete when the auctioneer announces its completion by the fall of the hammer, or in other customary manner; and until the announcement is made any bidder may retract his bid.

(3) A sale by auction may be notified to be subject to a reserve or upset price, and a right to bid may also be reserved expressly by or on behalf of the seller.

(4) Where a sale by auction is not notified to be subject to a right to bid by or on behalf of the seller, it is not lawful for the seller to bid himself or to employ any person to bid at the sale, or for the auctioneer knowingly to take any bid from the seller or any such person.

(5) A sale contravening subsection (4) above may be treated as fraudulent by the buyer.

(6) Where, in respect of a sale by auction, a right to bid is expressly reserved (but not otherwise) the seller or any one person on his behalf may bid at the auction.

Payment into court in Scotland.

58. In Scotland where a buyer has elected to accept goods which he might have rejected, and to treat a breach of contract as only giving rise to a claim for damages, he may, in an action by the seller for the price, be required, in the discretion of the court before which the action depends, to consign or pay into court the price of the goods, or part of the price, or to give other reasonable security for its due payment.

Reasonable time a question of fact.

59. Where a reference is made in this Act to a reasonable time the question what is a reasonable time is a question of fact.

60. Where a right, duty or liability is declared by this Act, it may (unless otherwise provided by this Act) be enforced by action. PART VII Rights etc. enforceable by action.

61.—(1) In this Act, unless the context or subject matter otherwise requires,— Interpretation.

" action " includes counterclaim and set-off, and in Scotland condescendence and claim and compensation ;

" business " includes a profession and the activities of any government department (including a Northern Ireland department) or local or public authority ;

" buyer " means a person who buys or agrees to buy goods ;

" contract of sale " includes an agreement to sell as well as a sale ;

" credit-broker " means a person acting in the course of a business of credit brokerage carried on by him, that is a business of effecting introductions of individuals desiring to obtain credit—

(*a*) to persons carrying on any business so far as it relates to the provision of credit, or

(*b*) to other persons engaged in credit brokerage ;

" defendant " includes in Scotland defender, respondent, and claimant in a multiplepoinding ;

" delivery " means voluntary transfer of possession from one person to another ;

" document of title to goods " has the same meaning as it has in the Factors Acts ;

" Factors Acts " means the Factors Act 1889, the Factors (Scotland) Act 1890, and any enactment amending or substituted for the same ; 1889 c. 45. 1890 c. 40

" fault " means wrongful act or default ;

" future goods " means goods to be manufactured or acquired by the seller after the making of the contract of sale ;

" goods " includes all personal chattels other than things in action and money, and in Scotland all corporeal moveables except money ; and in particular " goods " includes emblements, industrial growing crops, and things attached to or forming part of the land which are agreed to be severed before sale or under the contract of sale ;

" plaintiff " includes pursuer, complainer, claimant in a multiplepoinding and defendant or defender counter-claiming ;

PART VII

"property" means the general property in goods, and not merely a special property;

"quality", in relation to goods, includes their state or condition;

"sale" includes a bargain and sale as well as a sale and delivery;

"seller" means a person who sells or agrees to sell goods;

"specific goods" means goods identified and agreed on at the time a contract of sale is made;

"warranty" (as regards England and Wales and Northern Ireland) means an agreeement with reference to goods which are the subject of a contract of sale, but collateral to the main purpose of such contract, the breach of which gives rise to a claim for damages, but not to a right to reject the goods and treat the contract as repudiated.

(2) As regards Scotland a breach of warranty shall be deemed to be a failure to perform a material part of the contract.

(3) A thing is deemed to be done in good faith within the meaning of this Act when it is in fact done honestly, whether it is done negligently or not.

(4) A person is deemed to be insolvent within the meaning of this Act if he has either ceased to pay his debts in the ordinary course of business or he cannot pay his debts as they become due, whether he has committed an act of bankruptcy or not, and whether he has become a notour bankrupt or not.

(5) Goods are in a deliverable state within the meaning of this Act when they are in such a state that the buyer would under the contract be bound to take delivery of them.

(6) As regards the definition of "business" in subsection (1) above, paragraph 14 of Schedule 1 below applies in relation to a contract made on or after 18 May 1973 and before 1 February 1978, and paragraph 15 in relation to one made before 18 May 1973.

Savings: rules of law etc.

62.—(1) The rules in bankruptcy relating to contracts of sale apply to those contracts, notwithstanding anything in this Act.

(2) The rules of the common law, including the law merchant, except in so far as they are inconsistent with the provisions of this Act, and in particular the rules relating to the law of principal and agent and the effect of fraud, misrepresentation, duress or coercion, mistake, or other invalidating cause, apply to contracts for the sale of goods.

(3) Nothing in this Act or the Sale of Goods Act 1893 affects the enactments relating to bills of sale, or any enactment relating to the sale of goods which is not expressly repealed or amended by this Act or that. PART VII 1893 c. 71.

(4) The provisions of this Act about contracts of sale do not apply to a transaction in the form of a contract of sale which is intended to operate by way of mortgage, pledge, charge, or other security.

(5) Nothing in this Act prejudices or affects the landlord's right of hypothec or sequestration for rent in Scotland.

Consequential amendments, repeals and savings. 1978 c. 30.

63.—(1) Without prejudice to section 17 of the Interpretation Act 1978 (repeal and re-enactment), the enactments mentioned in Schedule 2 below have effect subject to the amendments there specified (being amendments consequential on this Act).

(2) The enactments mentioned in Schedule 3 below are repealed to the extent specified in column 3, but subject to the savings in Schedule 4 below.

(3) The savings in Schedule 4 below have effect.

Short title and commencement.

64.—(1) This Act may be cited as the Sale of Goods Act 1979.

(2) This Act comes into force on 1 January 1980.

UNFAIR CONTRACT TERMS ACT 1977 (C. 50)

Liability arising from sale or supply of goods

6.– (1) In the case of goods of a type ordinarily supplied for private use or consumption, where loss or damage – "Guarantee" of consumer goods

(a) arises from the goods proving defective while in consumer use; and

(b) results from the negligence of a person concerned in the manufacture or distribution of the goods,

liability for the loss or damage cannot be excluded or restricted by reference to any contract term or notice contained in or operating by reference to a guarantee of the goods.

(2) For these purposes–

(a) goods are to be regarded as "in consumer use" when a person is using them, or has them in his possession for use, otherwise than exclusively for the purposes of a business; and

(b) anything in writing is a guarantee if it contains or purports to contain some promise or assurance (however worded or presented) that defects will be made good by complete or partial replacement, or by repair, monetary compensation or otherwise.

(3) This section does not apply as between the parties to a contract under or in pursuance of which possession or ownership of the goods passed.

6.– (1) Liability for breach of the obligations arising from– Sale and hire-purchase

(a) section 12 of the Sale of Goods Act 1893 (seller's implied undertakings as to title, etc.); 56 & 57 Vict. c. 71.

(b) section 8 of the Supply of Goods (Implied Terms) Act 1973 (the corresponding thing in relation to hire-purchase), cannot be excluded or restricted by reference to any contract term.

(2) As against a person dealing as consumer, liability for breach of the obligations arising from—

(a) section 13, 14 or 15 of the 1893 Act (seller's implied undertakings as to conformity of goods with description or sample, or as to their quality or fitness for a particular purpose);

(b) section 9, 10 or 11 of the 1973 Act (the corresponding things in relation to hire-purchase),

cannot be excluded or restricted by reference to any contract term.

(3) As against a person dealing otherwise than as consumer, the liability specified in subsection (2) above can be excluded or restricted by reference to a contract term, but only in so far as the term satisfies the requirement of reasonableness.

(4) The liabilities referred to in this section are not only the business liabilities defined by section 1(3), but include those arising under any contract of sale of goods or hire-purchase agreement.

Miscellaneous contracts under which goods pass.

7.—(1) Where the possession or ownership of goods passes under or in pursuance of a contract not governed by the law of sale of goods or hire-purchase, subsections (2) to (4) below apply as regards the effect (if any) to be given to contract terms excluding or restricting liability for breach of obligation arising by implication of law from the nature of the contract.

(2) As against a person dealing as consumer, liability in respect of the goods' correspondence with description or sample, or their quality or fitness for any particular purpose, cannot be excluded or restricted by reference to any such term.

(3) As against a person dealing otherwise than as consumer, that liability can be excluded or restricted by reference to such a term, but only in so far as the term satisfies the requirement of reasonableness.

(4) Liability in respect of–

(a) the right to transfer ownership of the goods, or give possession; or

(b) the assurance of quiet possession to a person taking goods in pursuance of the contract,

cannot be excluded or restricted by reference to any such term except in so far as the term satisfies the requirement of reasonableness.

(5) This section does not apply in the case of goods passing on a redemption of trading stamps within the Trading Stamps Act 1964 or the Trading Stamps Act (Northern Ireland) 1965.

11.–(2) In determining for the purposes of section 6 or 7 above whether a contract term satisfies the requirement of reasonableness, regard shall be had in particular to the matters specified in Schedule 2 to this Act; but this subsection does not prevent the court or arbitrator from holding, in accordance with any rule of law, that a term which purports to exclude or restrict any relevant liability is not a term of the contract.

(4) Where by reference to a contract term or notice a person seeks to restrict liability to a specified sum of money, and the question arises (under this or any other Act) whether the term or notice satisfies the requirement of reasonableness, regard shall be had in particular (but without prejudice to subsection (2) above in the case of contract terms) to–

(a) the resources which he could expect to be available to him for the purpose of meeting the liability should it arise; and

(b) how far is was open to him to cover himself by insurance.

(5) It is for those claiming that a contract term or notice satisfies the requirement of reasonableness to show that it does.

"Dealing as consumer".

12.–(1) A party to a contract "deals as consumer" in relation to another party if–

(a) he neither makes the contract in the course of a business nor holds himself out as doing so; and

(b) the other party does make the contract in the course of a business; and

(c) in the case of a contract governed by the law of sale of goods or hire-purchase, or by section 7 of this Act, the goods passing under or in pursuance of the contract are of a type ordinarily supplied for private use or consumption.

(2) But on a sale by auction or by competitive tender the buyer is not in any circumstances to be regarded as dealing as consumer.

(3) Subject to this, it is for those claiming that a party does not deal as consumer to show that he does not.

13.–(1) To the extent that this Part of this Act prevents the exclusion or restriction of any liability it also prevents–

(a) making the liability or its enforcement subject to restrictive or onerous conditions;

(b) excluding or restricting any right or remedy in respect of the liability, or subjecting a person to any prejudice in consequence of his pursuing any such right or remedy;

(c) excluding or restricting rules of evidence or procedure; and (to that extent) sections 2 and 5 to 7 also prevent excluding or restricting liability by reference to terms and notices which exclude or restrict the relevant obligation or duty.

(2) But an agreement in writing to submit present or

future differences to arbitration is not to be treated under this Part of this Act as excluding or restricting any liability.

SCHEDULE 2

"Guidelines" for application of reasonableness test

The matters to which regard is to be had in particular for the purposes of sections 6(3), 7(3) and (4), 20 and 21 are any of the following which appear to be relevant—

(a) the strength of the bargaining positions of the parties relative to each other, taking into account (among other things) alternative means by which the customer's requirements could have been met;

(b) whether the customer received an inducement to agree to the term, or in accepting it had an opportunity of entering into a similar contract with other persons, but without having to accept a similar term;

(c) whether the customer knew or ought reasonably to have known of the existence and extent of the term (having regard, among other things, to any custom of the trade and any previous course of dealing between the parties);

(d) where the term excludes or restricts any relevant liability if some condition is not complied with, whether it was reasonable at the time of the contract to expect that compliance with that condition would be practicable;

(e) whether the goods were manufactured, processed or adapted to the special order of the customer.

Notes

1. An obvious area of difficulty which is not, however, dealt with is the *nemo dat* rule. This seemed to fit more conveniently into the proposed title on credit transactions.
2. Some civil law jurisdictions do actually have separate bodies of law for commercial and consumer contracts.
3. Compare Uniform Commercial Code (1972 text) 2-102: 'This article applies to transactions in goods.'
4. See e.g. *Chappell & Co. Ltd* v. *Nestlé* [1960] AC 87.
5. See *Aldridge* v. *Johnson* (1857) 7 E. & B. 885 the obligation being otherwise to pay a reasonable price – s. 8(2).
6. See *Young & Marten Ltd* v. *McManus Childs Ltd*, p. 102 below.
7. S. 4, Sale of Goods Act 1893, replacing s. 17 Statute of Frauds, 1677: for the historical reasons for this requirement see Holdsworth 6 H.E.L. 387 *et seq*.
8. Law Reform (Enforcement of Contracts) Act 1954.
9. [1935] 1 K.B. 579.
10. See text above.
11. See *Appleby* v. *Sleep* [1968] 1 WLR 948; *Pfizer Corpn* v. *Min. of Health* [1965] A.C. 512.
12. See *Head (Phillip) Ltd* v. *Showfronts Ltd* [1970] 1 Ll. Rep. 140.
13. See chapter 5, p. 51.
14. See *Fenwick* v. *MacDonald Fraser & Co* (1904) 6 F. 850 (Court of Session).
15. See S. Macaulay *Law, the Balance of Power* (Russell Sage Foundation, 1966).
16. See J. Adams, *Consideration for Requirements Contracts* [1932] 94 L.Q.R. 73.
17. [1934] 2 K.B. 1. Also *Hillas* v. *Arcros* [1932] All E.R. Rep. 494, and Uniform Commercial Code (1972 text) 2-305.
18. [1971] 1 WLR 803.
19. See *Griffiths* v. *Brymer* [1903] 2 K.B. 740 for an example of this approach outside sale of goods; but it may be that in other contracts frustration is more readily applied – see Treitel, *Law of Contract*, 5th edn. (Stevens, 1979), p. 684.
20. See the judgment of Lord Denning M.R. in *The Eugenia* [1964] 2 Q.B. 226, 238.
21. (1856) 5 H.L.C. 673. This case is generally said to be embodied in s. 6. The principle of the case, however, seems rather to be that embodied in s. 28 – payment and delivery are concurrent conditions. See Slade, [1954] 70 L.Q.R. 396.
22. 25 N.W. 42 (1885) Supreme Court of Wisconsin.
23. (1947) 177 L.T. 189.
24. O.W. Holmes, *The Common Law* (Little, Brown & Co., 1881), p. 298.
25. See e.g. *Tarling* v. *Baxter* (1827) 6 B & C 360. The same position would arise where the seller had an unpaid seller's lien over the goods (ss. 38, 39 and 41).

26. See section 2-509, Comment 1.
27. See Chapter 6, p. 115, on buyer's right of rejection.
28. See s. 20(2), Sale of Goods Act.
29. See C. Schmitthoff, *The Export Trade* (Sweet & Maxwell, 1980), p. 16.
30. [1923] 2 K.B. 500. See also *Karflex* v. *Poole* [1933] 2 K.B. 251.
31. See *Butterworth* v. *Kingsway Motors Ltd* [1954] 1 W.L.R. 1286.
32. See A.M. Honoré, *Oxford Essays in Jurisprudence* 1st series, A.G. Guest (ed.) (Oxford University Press, 1961).
33. See *Battersby and Preston* [1972] 35 M.L.R. 268.
34. This term covers patents, trade marks, copyright and designs, and some would say trade secrets and know-how.
35. [1975] 1 All E.R. 529.
36. SS. 13-15.
37. [1932] A.C. 562.
38. *Chandelor* v. *Lopus* (1603) Cro. Jac. 4; *Furnis* v. *Leicester* (1619) Cro. Jac. 474.
39. (1778) 1 Doug. 18.
40. From *Medina* v. *Stoughton* (1699) 1 Salk. 210, 1 Ld. Raym. 593.
41. *Gardiner* v. *Gray* (1815) 4 Camp. 144.
42. *Jones* v. *Bright* (1829) 5 Bing. 533.
43. *Derry* v. *Peek* (1899) 14 App. Cas. 337.
44. *Winterbottom* v. *Wright* (1842) 10 M & W 109. Two awkward cases providing exceptions to this rule were *Langridge* v. *Levy* (1837) 2 M & W 519; *George* v. *Skivington* (1869) L.R. 5 Ex 1.
45. [1932] A.C. 562.
46. Unless any written 'guarantee' or advertisement forms the basis of a collateral contract: see *Shanklin Pier Ltd* v. *Detel Products Ltd* [1951] 2 K.B. 854.
47. See *Young & Marten* v. *McManus*, p. 102, below.
48. Holmes, *The Common Law*, p. 298.
49. I.e. that the liability is the same as it is often held to be in hire contracts. See Law Commission Working Paper No. 71, para. 48 *et seq*.
50. *Goldberg* v. *Kollsman Instrument Corpn*, p. 100, below.
51. 2-318, p. 97, below.
52. S. 14(2), Sale of Goods Act 1893.
53. *Grant* v. *Australian Knitting Mills* [1936] A.C. 85, at p. 100.
54. As to the history of this provision, see Lord Wilberforce's speech in *Ashington Piggeries* v. *Christopher Hill* [1972] A.C. 441, 494.
55. See *Kendall* v. *Lillico* per Lord Reid, p. 64, below.
56. S. 14(1), Sale of Goods Act 1893.
57. See *Wren* v. *Holt* [1903] 1 K.B. 610: *Daniels* v. *White*, p. 94, below.
58. The important thing to remember is that s. 14(3) (fitness for purpose) was s. 14(1).
59. It is not to be supposed, however, that before the nineteenth century the activities of sellers was entirely unchecked. The presence or absence of a civil remedy was not (as it is not today) the most important control on sellers.
60. *Brown* v. *Craiks* (p. 79, below) is a very good illustration of this tension.
61. A justification for this approach is that once you allow parties to argue that what was contemplated was something other than the ordinary, you destroy the certainty of bargains. The counter to this is that it is often difficult to establish as an objective fact what the ordinary is anyway.
62. *The Theory of Legal Interpretation* (1899) 12 H.L.R. 417, 420.
63. See the first-instance decision in *Cehave* v. *Bremer Handelsgesellschaft*,

p. 116, below.
64. [1933] AC 470.
65. [1921] 2 K.B. 519.
66. [1972] A.C. 441, 502, and see extract at pp. 78 et seq, below. See also *Vacwell Engineering Co.* v. *B.D.H. Chemicals*, p. 83, below; *Kendall* v. *Lillico*, p. 64, below.
67. Temores, when he sacked Sebastia, promised that no blood would be shed. He buried the inhabitants alive. This was naughty.
68. See Law Commission Report No. 82 Cmnd. 6831, *Liability for Defective Products*.
69. On durability, see *Broome* v. *Pandess Co-operative Society* [1940] 1 All E.R. 603: *Mash & Murrell Ltd* v. *Jos. I. Emmanuel* [1961] 1 All E.R. 485: *Cordova Land Co.* v. *Victor Bros* [1966] 1 W.L.R. 793: *Crowther* v. *Shannon Motor Co.* [1975] 1 W.L.R. 30: Law Commission Working Paper No. 71.
70. Equivalent to s. 14(3), Sale of Goods Act 1979.
71. Equivalent to s. 14(2), Sale of Goods Act 1979.
72. (1955) 123 N.E. 2d 792.
73. (1872) L.R. 7 Ex. 111.
74. See *Hyman* v. *Nye* (1881) 6 Q.B.D. 685.
75. As to the meaning of this term, see Fuller and Perdue, *The Reliance Interest in Contract Damages* [1936] 46 Y.L.J. 52: *Ogus on Damages* (Butterworths, 1973), Ch. VIII. Roughly, the expectation interest is the expected profit or gain from the deal. When the sellers sell at a loss, the price nevertheless represents their maximum gain under the contract.
76. (1853) 2 E.B. 678.
77. *Roth* v. *Tayson* (1896) 73 L.T. 628.
78. *Melachrino* v. *Nicholl & Knight* [1920] 1 K.B. 693.
79. [1962] A.C. 413, 431.
80. See *Vitex Manufacturing Corp.* v. *Caribtex Corp.* 377 F. 2d. 795 (1967) United States Court of Appeals 3rd Circuit.
81. 194 F. 2d. 859 (1952) United States Court of Appeals 3rd Circuit.
82. [1966] C.L.J. 192, 194.
83. See *Borrowman, Phillips & Co.* v. *Free & Hollis* (1878) 4 Q.B.D. 500; *E.E. & Brian Smith (1928) Ltd* v. *Wheatsheaf Mills Ltd* [1939] 2 K.B. 302.
84. See *Parsons* v. *Uttley*, p. 132, below.
85. The principle seems to have emerged from the tortious actions of detinue and trover. It was thrust on the reluctant Scots in *Dunlop* v. *Higgins* (1848) 1 H.L.C. 381.
86. For a case where the string became a loop see *Williams* v. *Agius* [1914] A.C. 510.
87. See the modification of this formulation in *Koufos* v. *Czarnikow Ltd* [1969] A.C. 350.
88. See Albery [1975] 91 L.Q.R. 337.
89. P.S. Atiyah, *The Sale of Goods*, 5th edn. (Pitman, 1980), p. 308.
90. See *Parsons* v. *Uttley*, p. 132, below.
91. See 2-708 Uniform Commercial Code (1978 text).
92. [1955] Ch. 177.
93. *Chart* v. *Sullivan* [1957] 2 A.C. 117.
94. For the same reason, s. 4, which deals with indemnities and s. 9, which seeks to regulate the consequences of a fundamental breach on an otherwise operative clause, are omitted. On indemnities, see Adams' and Brownsword's forthcoming articles in the *Journal of Business Law*.

Index

For Product Safety Concerns and Information please contact our EU
representative GPSR@taylorandfrancis.com
Taylor & Francis Verlag GmbH, Kaufingerstraße 24, 80331 München, Germany

www.ingramcontent.com/pod-product-compliance
Ingram Content Group UK Ltd.
Pitfield, Milton Keynes, MK11 3LW, UK
UKHW020205200926
475702UK00004B/625
9781032005348